Thomas Babington (Lord) Macaulay (1800–1859)
History of England from the Accession of James II
(1848–1861)

John Burrow is one of Britain's leading intellectual historians. He was Professor of Intellectual History at the University of Sussex from 1981 to 1995, and Professor of European Thought at the University of Oxford from 1995 to 2000. His books include *Evolution and Society: A Study in Victorian Social Theory* (1996); *A Liberal Descent: Victorian Historians and the English Past* (1981), awarded the Wolfson Prize for History; *Gibbon* (1984); *The Crisis of Reason: European Thought, 1884–1914* (2000); and *A History of Histories: Epics, Chronicles, Romances and Inquiries from Herodotus and Thucydides to the Twentieth Century* (2007). He is a Fellow of the British Academy, and an Emeritus Fellow of Balliol College, Oxford.

CONTINUUM HISTORIES
The greatest narrative history writing in English

This series is designed to attract a new generation of readers to some of the greatest narrative history ever written. Each volume includes a dramatic episode from a major work of history, prefaced with an introduction by a leading modern authority.

Continuum Histories demonstrate the extraordinary tradition that exists of great history writing in the English language – and that often the best stories are true stories.

Series Editor: Mark Bostridge

History
of England

Also in Continuum Histories

William H. Prescott's *History of the Conquest of Mexico*.
Introduced and selected by J.H. Elliott

J.A. Froude's *The Reign of Mary Tudor*.
Introduced and selected by Eamon Duffy

Edward Gibbon's *Decline and Fall of the Roman Empire*.
Introduced and selected by Tom Holland (forthcoming)

Thomas Carlyle's *The French Revolution*.
Introduced and selected by Ruth Scurr (forthcoming)

LORD MACAULAY

History of England

Introduced and selected by
John Burrow

continuum

Published by the Continuum International Publishing Group

The Tower Building   80 Maiden Lane
11 York Road   Suite 704
London   New York
SE1 7NX   NY 10038

www.continuumbooks.com

First published 2009

British Library Cataloguing-in-Publication Data
A catalogue record for this book is available from the British Library.

ISBN 978-1441-13374-8

Designed and typeset by www.benstudios.co.uk
Printed and bound by the MPG Books Group

CONTENTS

INTRODUCTION

When he was planning his *History* Macaulay wrote confidently, 'I really think that posterity will not willingly let my book die'.[1] His confidence was amply justified. *The History of England in the Reigns of James II and William III* is, however, only a fragment of what Macaulay planned as a much longer work, which would end only in his own lifetime. It would have led, as Macaulay said, from the Revolution of 1688, which brought the crown into harmony with Parliament, to the 1832 Reform Act, in whose passage he had played a notable part as a Whig MP, whose extension of the franchise brought Parliament into harmony with the nation.[2] Macaulay died in 1859, with only the part of the *History* up to the end of the reign of William III completed. The earlier part had, however, already achieved an extraordinary popularity when the opening volumes appeared in 1848. Macaulay was a celebrated essayist and Parliamentary orator, with an official career in India behind him as a member of its governing council, which, though it lasted only four years, procured him financial independence for life. His political career continued after he returned, and led to a peerage, but his attention was increasingly given to his *History*.

Macaulay's published essays, second only in reputation to the *History*, are vigorous, sparkling performances, begun when he was a young man in the 1820s. It was through these, mainly in the Whig journal the *Edinburgh Review*, and through his speeches in the House of Commons on the Parliamentary Reform Bill in the early 1830s, that Macaulay first made his name. He was in many respects, in culture, temperament and career, the last of the great classical and neo-classical historians, who wrote the history of public events and personalities after holding high public offices. Many, from Polybius in the second century BC, to Viscount Bolingbroke in the eighteenth century, had regarded such a career as indispensable to a historian. Three Whig politicians in the early nineteenth century, Charles James Fox, Lord John Russell and Sir James Mackintosh – from whom Macaulay inherited a valuable collection of seventeenth-century pamphlets – had already written on 'The Glorious Revolution', as Whig tradition had come to call it.

Macaulay was well aware of his links with the ancient historians. 'The truth is', he wrote in his journal (7 December 1849), 'I admire no historian much except Herodotus, Thucydides and Tacitus'. Modern historians, Hume, Robertson, Gibbon, Voltaire, had only 'merit'.[3] He felt a sense of kinship with Livy, whose re-telling of early Roman legends provided inspiration for his bravura narrative poems *The Lays of Ancient Rome*. His own culture was essentially classical, though he was also thoroughly familiar with the European literature of the eighteenth century. He continued to read the Greek and Latin classics throughout his life.

To Macaulay, after, as an undergraduate in Cambridge, he shed his father's Toryism and fervent Evangelical

Christianity, Whiggism was the foundation of his creed, though as always such a capacious term needs elaboration. Though he moved as a young man in the circle of the followers of Fox, he admired Burke more and despised the republican theoreticians of the seventeenth century as impractical and arrogant would-be oligarchs, as he did their later counterparts in the French Revolution. His own Whiggism was bourgeois, incorporating enthusiasm for material progress and combining zeal for reform with veneration for England's long constitutional past. Whiggism stood for practical and moderate innovation, not doctrinaire panaceas. It combined progress with stability, which in the 1820s, when Macaulay entered politics, meant a cautiously enlarged franchise, administrative reform and the removal of the civil disabilities imposed on Catholics and Nonconformists, which were a legacy of the repressive legislation of seventeenth-century Anglican parliaments, fearful of Rome and hostile to Dissent. His *History* has much to say on this; in it his commitment to religious freedom was tempered by his belief that James II's Catholicism, combined with aspirations to an autocracy like that of Louis XIV, was then a real danger to constitutional liberty.

Overt political partisanship in the *History* is muted by a sense that ultimately the interest of the population as a whole, in order and constitutional rule, transcended religious animosities and at moments of crisis was felt to do so. He therefore particularly celebrates the moments when, in 1688, the nation could be seen rallying in defence of its inherited freedoms and coming together to thwart James' arbitrariness, and then to avert anarchy after his flight had left the country without a legitimate government. Readers could have had no doubt, of course, that the author of the *History* was a Whig, nor did Macaulay intend them to. Whiggism, for him, was an almost perennial element in English history, antedating the adoption of the political labels Whig and Tory in the later seventeenth century. He told the Edinburgh electors so in 1839, when he was soliciting their votes and affirming his political allegiance:

> It seems to me that when I look back on our history, I can discern a great party which has, through many generations, preserved its identity … a party which, though often tainted with the faults of the age, has always been in advance of the age … [and] has the glory of having established our civil and religious liberties on a firm foundation.[4]

The ensuing historical survey offered by Macaulay began with the parliamentary opposition in the latter part of the reign of Elizabeth and ended with the reforms of his own day, some of them passed under a Tory government: election speeches cannot be expected to emulate the scrupulousness of history. In the *History* itself the manner is often vehement; Macaulay's is a prose that seeks to overwhelm rather than insinuate. He was one of the outstanding orators of his day and his syntax often employed the rhetorical device of repetition with variations ('a party which … a party which'). It was the insistence of a debater or barrister – Macaulay was called to the bar though he did not practise. The precedents of ancient historiography and oratory, in which he was steeped, often seem close to the surface. In the ancient world oratory and historical writing were closely allied arts.

These precedents were relevant too to Macaulay's portrayals of character, which often read like indictments, recalling the Roman genres of the invective and eulogy, though they were also typical of the historiography of his own age, which seldom missed the opportunity to moralize. A colourful example is his contemptuous dismissal of the radical pamphleteer and agitator Robert Ferguson, who represented for him all that was worst in seventeenth-century Whiggism. 'Violent, malignant, regardless of truth, insensible to shame, insatiable of notoriety, delighting in intrigue, in tumult, in mischief for its own sake, he toiled many years in the deepest mines of faction' (ch. V). He was 'a low minded agitator, half maniac and half knave' (ch. IX).

At the other end of the political spectrum, the adventurers who made up James' associates are drawn with similar emphasis. The most memorable of all is the notorious Chief Justice Jeffries, whose end is described (below, p. 123) with particular relish. Jeffries' cruelty was already a Whig legend, which Macaulay inscribed indelibly for posterity in a florid portrait of terrifying savagery, judicial sadism and drunken buffoonery.

> Impudence and ferocity sat on his brow. The glare of his eyes had a fascination for the unhappy victim on whom they were fixed. Yet his brow and eye were less terrible than the savage lines of his mouth. His yell of fury, as was said by one who had often heard it, sounded like the thunder of the judgement day. (ch. IV)

To enter his court, Macaulay said, was to enter the den of a wild beast. In dealing with the accused rebels – Macaulay exaggerates the number of his victims – after the Western rising, Jeffries was in his element: 'He stormed, cursed and swore in language which no wellbred man would have used at a race or a cockfight'. Jeffries' robust characterizations of the connection between religious dissent and treason were sufficient warning not to expect judicial impartiality: 'There is not one of those lying, snivelling, canting Presbyterians but, one way or another, had a hand in the rebellion. Presbytery has all manner of villainy in it.' When the clergyman preaching the Assize sermon at Dorchester spoke of the duty of mercy, 'the ferocious mouth of the Judge was distended in an ominous grin'. To one victim he said, 'I see thee villain. I see thee already with the halter around thy neck'. His spirits, Macaulay says, rose higher and higher as the work went on. 'He laughed, shouted, joked and swore in such a way that many thought him drunk from morning till night. But in him it was not easy to distinguish the madness produced by evil passions from the madness produced by brandy' (ch. V).

Macaulay's manner inclined to vehemence, but his understanding of politics and history was essentially moderate, pragmatic and reconciliatory. He saw Restoration England as a society corrupted by despotism and cheerfully took on the role of its satirist, as though he had been Juvenal or Tacitus. William of Orange, for him, amply deserved his title of 'The Deliverer'. Most of Macaulay's heroes were men like himself, men of fluency, disputation and rhetorical energy. He speaks with reverence of great seventeenth-century lawyers like Maynard, or great parliamentary speakers like Somers (below, p. 56), a young arriviste like himself from a modest background, whose talents made him a great lord; today they are not even names except to historians. But William was something else; a strong, reticent, stoical man, overcoming frail health in his dedication of his lifetime's purpose; the preservation of his country's independence. Macaulay rather glosses over the fact that his country was the United Provinces and that to him Britain mattered essentially as an ally to be thrown into the European balance to frustrate Louis XIV's drive to hegemony for France. The consequent involvement of Britain in a protracted continental war became a cause of bitter political division.

But Macaulay had no doubt that William had served Britain supremely well. It was only through his intervention that the constitutional role of Parliament could be made lastingly secure. Britain needed William as much as William needed Britain. According to Macaulay he cleansed and held together a corrupted nation that would otherwise probably have succumbed to faction and despotism. But Macaulay also stressed in his narrative that Englishmen had been accomplices in their own deliverance: the peers who invited William; the Dissenters who refused to be bribed by an illegal offer of religious toleration into support for James' despotism; the clergy who declined to read the Declaration of Indulgence; the bishops who supported them and the jury that acquitted the bishops, and even the mobs that celebrated their verdict. In these events the future of England had hung in the balance. That is the critical theme of the sections printed here.

For Macaulay, as often for English Whigs the contrast was with France, which, suffering a 200-year hiatus in its constitutional development, was left by the end of the eighteenth century with no recourse but to a violently innovatory revolution. The 1688 Revolution and the 1832 Reform Act were the successive stages of England's preservation from such a fate. An ordered liberty, Macaulay had no doubt, was the guarantor of material progress. This contained a threat which could be averted by cautious but timely reform. As he admonished the House of Commons, the passage of the Reform Bill was essential to avert revolutionary catastrophe: 'The great cause of revolutions is this, that while nations move onwards, constitutions stand still.'[5] In pointing to the fatal discrepancy between social progress and constitutional immobility, Macaulay was echoing David Hume's history of Stuart England, written a century before, and even uses the same example. Charles I was doomed, Hume had told his readers and Macaulay now told the Commons, because he had failed to read the signs of the times: 'he would govern the men of the seventeenth century as if they had been the men of the sixteenth century.'[6]

What Macaulay was invoking here was a favourite conception of the Scottish Enlightenment which he made his own; 'the progress of civil society'. We have, in fact, to distinguish two strands in Macaulay's Whiggism: this one, alongside a Burkean conception of politics that was pragmatic and gradualist, respectful of tradition and precedent without being circumscribed by them. The conception of social change, far from licensing rapid constitutional transformation, required the most sensitive political tact to manage its consequences. Burke had proclaimed that the English way in politics was to weigh, balance and reconcile. Timeliness was everything because its reward was the preservation of continuity. 'Reform', Macaulay exhorted the Commons,

Reform that you may preserve. Now therefore, while everything at home and abroad forebodes ruin to those who persist in a hopeless struggle against the spirit of the age, now, while the crash of the proudest throne of the continent [in the French Revolution of 1830] is still resounding in our ears ... now, while old feelings and old associations retain a power and a charm which may soon pass away...[7]

Macaulay had no doubt that the spontaneous energies of a free people would inevitably further the growth of national prosperity. (The ancient historians would have agreed, though they would have spoken of military prowess rather than prosperity.) The opening of the *History* proclaimed that 'from the auspicious union of order and freedom sprang a prosperity of which the annals of human affairs had furnished no example'. For him the line from the accession to the throne of William and Mary to what we now call the industrial revolution and the wealth of Victorian England was a clear and straight one. That is why, though it attracted mockery, he thought it appropriate to celebrate William's landing in 1688 with an enthusiastic reminder of the bustle and opulence of modern Torbay, where 'the waves then broke on a desolate beach' (below, p. 90).

His delight in social and material progress is most fully displayed in the famous third chapter, with its repeated contrasts of the squalors of late Stuart England with the improvements of his own day. Again his predecessor was Hume, in a chapter in his Stuart history, which was later relegated to an appendix. The traditional term for such interpolations, going back to Herodotus, had been a 'digression', usually a description of the customs and manners of remote peoples, rather than Macaulay's contrasts of 'then' and 'now': here the remote and almost barbarous people were the inhabitants of late seventeenth-century England.

But Macaulay's chapter, though it became notorious, is not his main achievement. His *History* as a whole belongs squarely in the tradition of the classical histories he admired so much as a narrative of great public events. He was an unsurpassed impresario of history as dramatic action, laid out for his readers in a vivid, powerful energetic prose that made them almost spectators of stirring and colourful events in London and the provinces, in Parliament and the courts, in Scotland and Ireland. There were full accounts of the Argyll and Monmouth rebellions, the massacre at Glencoe, the siege of Londonderry. Macaulay referred to his work on the last as sewing on a purple patch. Restraint and qualification are not his forte, but, when that is accepted, what he offers is intensely engaging and exhilarating. He was a warm-blooded exuberant man, who responded to energy and bustle, and conveyed them. Predictably, he loved the 1851 Great Exhibition: 'a most gorgeous sight; vast, graceful, beyond the dreams of the Arabian romances'.[8] He responded also to scenes of pageantry. As an MP he had been able to attend the coronation of William IV in 1831. He dwells in a letter to his sister Hannah on its impressiveness: the grey pillars of Westminster Abbey set off by the blaze of scarlet and gold in robes and uniforms.[9] The description in the *History* (below, p. 162) of the proclamation of William and Mary surely owed something to his recollection of the later event.

Macaulay's handling of animated scenes, diversified by small vignettes, reminds one of Hogarth but perhaps still more of the teeming canvases of a contemporary artist like Frith; Derby Day, Ramsgate Sands, a busy railway station. James II, to overawe the capital and be ready for armed intervention, established a military camp at Hounslow on the edge of London. Macaulay's brief description ironically illustrates the subversion of James' design as the camp becomes a kind of fair:

> Mingled with the musketeers and dragoons, a multitude of fine gentlemen and ladies from Soho Square [then a fashionable district], sharpers and painted women from Whitefriars, invalids in sedans, monks in hoods and gowns, lacqueys in rich liveries, pedlars, orange girls, mischievous apprentices and gaping clowns [rustics] were constantly passing and repassing through the long lanes of tents. (ch. IV)

In the confrontation of the soldiers and the Londoners it is the latter, allegedly, who suborn the army, not *vice versa*, as the allurements of civil society prevail and the soldiers, enjoying themselves, cease to be intimidating. A different kind of relation of civil to military is the entry of William's army into Exeter, the first English city to receive him (below, p. 94). The army, potentially terrible, is actually, thanks to William, the guardian of an ordered liberty and stands for constitutional freedom supported by arms. Following his contemporary source, Macaulay's description recalls the taste for describing processions found earlier in Tudor chroniclers like Edward Hall.

Macaulay was above all at home, like Thucydides, with contests of eloquence. The momentous parliamentary or legal occasions, when an encroaching despotism is confronted by the assertion and exercise of inherited rights, call out his highest powers of exalted evocation. The trial of the bishops (below, pp. 54–66), in which the fortunes of the prosecution and defence sway one way and then the other, as in a football match, is one notable example. Another is one of Macaulay's most celebrated essays, on Warren Hastings, whose focal point is Hastings' impeachment, in the 1780s, for alleged abuse of the powers entrusted to him by the East India Company in far away Bengal.

The trial dragged on inconclusively and Macaulay admits it became a bore, but its opening is one of his most memorable epic set-pieces, with a Homeric roll-call of the participants and spectators, drawn together by an occasion worthy of them, an assertion of accountability to Parliament even of the mightiest subject:

All the talents and all the accomplishments which are developed by liberty and civilization were now displayed... The High Court of Parliament was to sit, according to forms handed down from the days of the Plantagenets, on an Englishman accused of exercising tyranny over the lord of the holy city of Benares.

The setting, Westminster Hall, was redolent of English history. It was:

the great hall of William Rufus, the hall which had resounded with acclamations at the inauguration of thirty kings ... the hall where Charles had confronted the High Court of Justice with the placid courage which has half redeemed his fame... The grey old walls were hung with scarlet. The long galleries were crowded by an audience such as has seldom excited the fears or the emulation of an orator...

The stage, the arts, literature were represented by the great actress Mrs Siddons, by Joshua Reynolds and by Gibbon. Fashionable society was headed by the Duchess of Devonshire. Among the accusers were Fox and Sheridan, who drew Macaulay into an Athenian allusion: 'The English Demosthenes and the English Hyperides'. The future was there, in the young Charles Grey, who was to be prime minister, over 30 years later, at the time of the passage of the Reform Bill. Above all there was the chief accuser, Edmund Burke. The stir made by his opening speech was such that 'Handkerchiefs were pulled out; smelling bottles were handed round; and Mrs Sheridan was carried out in a fit'.

Macaulay could not resist the touch of burlesque, but the grandeur was real, a high civilization, guided by ancient procedure, was lending its greatest talents to the service of its political and humane conscience. He was a connoisseur of oratory as well as an orator himself, and was happy to be the memorialist of the great performances of past generations: the folklore of the club, Parliament, of which he was proudly a member. Ancient historians, following Thucydides, had been in the habit of reporting speeches apparently verbatim. Their modern successors had become more inhibited about using direct speech without documentary warrant, and Macaulay was content to summarize the sense, but his accounts scarcely lose in vividness and impressiveness; the voice we hear is a blend of the speaker's and the historian's. As was also traditional, he did not shirk his obligations to battles and sieges, but the core of the *History* is civil, its moments of highest drama the great parliamentary and legal occasions he always sought to place in the long perspective of past performances and precedents, of history in the making. In a letter at the time, he spoke of hearing the result of the crucial vote on the Reform Bill announced at the bar of the House as being like seeing Caesar stabbed or Oliver Cromwell picking up the mace when he dismissed the Long Parliament.[10]

The sense of history was always alert in Macaulay, even on more trivial occasions. Among all the fascinations he found in the great London world of politics and high society in the early 1830s to which his talents had given him the entrée, the living mementoes of the eighteenth century had a special interest: Lord North's daughter, Charles James Fox's nephew, intimates of Horace Walpole, and the French minister Talleyrand, survivor of the Revolution. Macaulay was struck by the appearance of the Marquess Wellesley, Wellington's brother and former Governor in India: 'he has made a great and splendid figure in history... Such a blooming old swain I never saw... hair combed with exquisite nicety, – a waistcoat of driven snow and a star and garter put on with rare skill.'[11] All aspects of the human comedy were interesting to Macaulay, but most of all when they carried a fragrance of the past. It is noticeable that later, when he had returned from India and was himself moving into an older generation, current affairs seemed to attract him less than getting on with his *History*.

The most momentous of parliamentary occasions in the *History* involved an ad hoc body, not a constitutionally summoned Parliament. Its deliberations (below, p. 129) settled the vexed question of the Succession, James having fled, which it resolved with the offer of the crown jointly to William and Mary. The nation, which had hovered on the verge of anarchy, was rescued by a common will to order, no matter at what cost is consistency and transparency, transcending profound political disagreements. In his essay 20 years earlier on the Whig constitutional historian Hallam, Macaulay had dwelt even more emphatically than he did now on the intellectual poverty of the debates, the sacrifice of lucidity and principle to legalistic quibbling, antiquarian citations of precedent and a shameless resort to fiction. But one of the historical lessons passed on by the Scottish Enlightenment had been a paradox: weakness and even vice were sometimes useful, and there was no direct correlation between moral worth in actions and their performers and the beneficence of their results. This has come to be called the idea of 'unintended consequences'. To take an example used by Macaulay and others, Henry VIII's divorce and the Dissolution of the Monasteries and the politic time-serving to which the Church of England owed its origin might be morally shabby but were historically beneficial. The same point had been made by Hume about the fanaticism of seventeenth-century Puritans, which had nerved them to resist despotism as nothing else could have done.[12] Macaulay exploited the idea to full ironic effect in his account of the proceedings of 1688. He wrote in 'Hallam' that 'it was fortunate for our civil government that the Revolution was in great measure effected by men who cared little about their political principles'. Flexibility and willingness to compromise, not logic and principled intransigence, were what the situation required. At such a crisis 'splendid talents and strong passions might have done more harm than good.'

The ominous counter-example, as always, was France, which showed what harm might have ensued. It was well that the English Revolution had, as it were, denied its own character as a revolution, and been conducted with the most sensitive regard to precedent and ancient traditions, as when the new sovereigns – sovereign, in fact, by parliamentary vote – were proclaimed with all the old pageantry (below, p. 162). The antique façade was functional and worth preserving. The alternative was the tabula rasa confronted by the French National Assembly. In England the Revolution gave no license to indefinite, unresolved political experimentation in a permanently unsettled figure: 'To us, who have lived in the year 1848, it may seem almost an abuse of terms to call a proceeding conducted with so much minute attention to prescriptive etiquette by the terrible name of Revolution' (below, p. 170).

It is instructive to compare Macaulay with another mid-Victorian who exploited even more explicitly the paradox of a constitution that worked although – or rather because – it was a sham: Walter Bagehot in *The English Constitution* (1865). Bagehot surely owes something to Macaulay's essays, which he cites frequently, and to Burke and to the Scottish Enlightenment. But compared with Macaulay's, his formulation of the central Whig paradox ('it is necessary to keep up the ancient show while we interpolate the new reality')[13] makes a much greater impression of cynicism; his characteristic manner is a sophisticated knowingness with none of Macaulay's spontaneous complicity with an imposing fiction. For Bagehot the mark, and one might even say the virtue, of a free polity was its reassuring dullness. For Macaulay, as his *History* amply demonstrates, a historically grounded liberty was a sublime thing and its exercise rose at times to the dignity of epic. The balance between knowingness and reverence is held in Macaulay, and the account of the proclamation of William and Mary is both ironic and impressively grand; it would be possible to miss the irony altogether. Invocations of divine Providence are rarer in Macaulay than in some of his contemporaries, though chapter X ends with one (below, p. 179), but he can sometimes remind us of an older, reverent version of 'unintended consequences' in which Providence habitually makes use of feeble and erring human agents to accomplish its benign ends.

Macaulay clearly enjoys his knowingness, and shares it with his sophisticated readers: the weaknesses of the framers of the Revolution Settlement were by an historical irony their strength. But he also clearly enjoys – one might say participates, in a way Bagehot never does – in the ancient pageantry and the attention to 'prescriptive etiquette', as well as endorsing their consequences. A common jubilation, not a covert smile, is what he invites his readers to share. What we are witnessing is the immediate salvation and long-term preservation of England from a revolution *á la française*. Macaulay's work is unique in the intensity and lucidity with which he unites the opposed characteristics of irony and celebration. His politics was pragmatic and down to earth; an acre in Middlesex, he liked saying, is preferable to a kingdom in utopia. But when he came to present it as embodied in England's past, it was a pragmatism proudly announced by heralds in an exultant fanfare of trumpets.

John Burrow

SUGGESTIONS FOR FURTHER READING

Burrow, John, *A History of Histories* (London: Allen Lane, 2007). Part V, chapters 21 and 22. Details more fully the relations between Macaulay and Hume.

Clive, John, *Macaulay: The Shaping of the Historian* (London: Secker & Warburg, 1973). Particularly helpful on Macaulay's early views and their connections with English History.

Thomas, William, *The Quarrel of Macaulay and Croker: Politics and History in the Age of Reform* (Oxford: Oxford University Press, 2000). A subtle study of a contemporary controversy and the personalities involved in it.

Trevelyan, George Otto, *The Life and Letters of Lord Macaulay* (London: Longmans, Green, Spottiswoode, 1876). One of the great Victorian biographies, by Macaulay's nephew.

NOTES

1. G.O. Trevelyan, *The Life and Letters of Lord Macaulay* (London: Longmans, Green, Spottiswoode, 1876), p. 364.

2. Thomas Pinney (ed.), *The Letters of Thomas Babington Macaulay* (6 vols, Cambridge: Cambridge University Press, 1974–81), III, p. 252.

3. Trevelyan, *Life and Letters*, pp. 533–4.

4. *The Miscellaneous Writings and Speeches of Lord Macaulay* (London: Longman, Green and Co., 1889), p. 583.

5. *Miscellaneous Writings*, p. 496.

6. *Miscellaneous Writings*, 526. See David Hume, *The History of Great Britain* (ed. Duncan Forbes, London: Penguin Books, 1970), especially p. 381.

7. *Miscellaneous Writings*, p. 492.

8. Trevelyan, *Life and Letters*, p. 551.

9. Pinney (ed.), *Letters*, II, pp. 97–9.

10. Pinney (ed.), *Letters*, II, p. 9.

11. Pinney (ed.), *Letters*, II, pp. 258–9.

12. Hume, *The History of Great Britain*, pp. 466–7, pp. 502–3

13. Walter Bagehot, *The English Constitution* in Norman St John Stevas (ed.), *The Collected Works of Walter Bagehot*, (15 vols, London: The Economist, 1965–86), V, p. 392. Bagehot's use elsewhere of a phrase unimaginable in Macaulay measures the distance between the two writers: 'historical twaddle about the rise of British liberty'. Bagehot, *Works*, VI, p. 99.

HISTORY
OF ENGLAND

The nation Macaulay describes, from the defeat of the Monmouth rebellion in the first year of James II's reign in 1685 (chapter V), is one made increasingly anxious and irritated by the King's attempts to favour Roman Catholics, by installing them in offices legally barred to them by legislation in the previous reign, enacted by a parliament determined to secure the monopoly of the Church of England over such appointments. Both Catholics and Protestant Dissenters had been made marginal to national life and impeded in the public practice of their religion. James also caused much alarm by his steps to establish a standing army, largely composed of Irish Catholics, which could be used as an instrument of coercion under his own personal control. A standing army was anathema to both Whigs and Tories, carrying recollections of Cromwell's military rule.

In the first two chapters selections from which are printed here (VII and VIII), Macaulay describes opposition to James' policies rising to a climax with the King's Declaration of Indulgence, issued under the royal perogative, to both Catholics and Dissenters. Seven Anglican bishops were prosecuted as a result of their refusal to publicize the Declaration and were acquitted amid immense public enthusiasm. The Declaration, which in effect annulled a recent Act of Parliament (the Test Act 1673), was regarded by both Whigs and Tories as illegal. The position of the Tories, however, was peculiarly difficult: torn between their fundamental principles of loyalty to the crown, to the constitution and the Church of England by the actions of a Catholic monarch apparently determined to use unconstitutional means to subvert the established church. To the Dissenters James' Declaration represented a temptation and perhaps a trap. They could take the bait of relief only on condition of similar relief for Catholics, whom they, like many

23

others, typically regarded as national enemies and whom James clearly intended not merely to tolerate but to promote to key positions. The Declaration also represented a usurpation of the parliamentary sovereignty which many of their fathers and grandfathers had fought for in the Civil War.

In Chapter IX we have the secret invitation by a handful of peers to the King's son-in-law, William Prince of Orange, to land in England in defence of the constitution and the Protestant religion. William invades, and the nation's leaders, after initial hesitation, rally to him and James flees from Whitehall. Chapter X, the crux of the whole History, *recounts the debates over the various constitutional options, ending with the joint proclamation of William and his wife, James' elder daughter Mary, as joint sovereigns.*

Later chapters, not printed here, cover the next reign: the imposition of the revolutionary settlement on Scotland and Ireland and its consolidating legislation, the war with France and the unsuccessful Jacobite attempts to overthrow William with French backing.

HISTORY

The original purpose of James had been to obtain for the Church of which he was a member, not only complete immunity from all penalties and from all civil disabilities, but also an ample share of ecclesiastical and academical endowments, and at the same time to enforce with rigour the laws against the Puritan sects.

It seemed clear that, if he effected his purpose, he must effect it in defiance of that great party which had given such signal proofs of fidelity to his office, to his family, and to his person. The whole Anglican priesthood, the whole Cavalier gentry, were against him. In vain had he, by virtue of his ecclesiastical supremacy, enjoined the clergy to abstain from discussing controverted points. Every parish in the nation was warned every Sunday against the errors of Rome; and these warnings were only the more effective because they were accompanied by professions of reverence for the Sovereign, and of a determination to endure with patience whatever it might be his pleasure to inflict. The royalist knights and esquires who, through forty-five years of war and faction, had stood so manfully by the throne, now expressed, in no measured phrase, their resolution to stand as manfully by the Church. Dull as was the intellect of James, despotic as was his temper, he felt that he must change his course. He could not safely venture to outrage all his Protestant subjects at once. If he could bring himself to make concessions to the party which predominated in both Houses, if he could bring himself to leave to the established religion all its dignities, emoluments, and privileges unimpaired, he might still break up Presbyterian meetings, and fill the gaols with Baptist preachers. But, if he was determined to plunder the hierarchy, he must make up his mind to forego the luxury of persecuting the Dissenters.

But it was only by slow degrees and after many struggles that the King could prevail on himself to form an alliance with all that he most abhorred. He had to overcome an animosity, not slight or capricious, not of recent origin or hasty growth, but hereditary in his line, strengthened by great wrongs inflicted and suffered through a hundred and twenty eventful years, and intertwined with all his feelings, religious, political, domestic, and personal. Four generations of Stuarts had waged a war to the death with four generations of Puritans; and, through that long war, there had been no Stuart who had hated the Puritans so much, or who had been so much hated by them, as himself. They had tried to blast his honour and to exclude him from his birthright; they had called him incendiary, cutthroat, poisoner: they had driven him from the Admiralty and the Privy Council: they had repeatedly chased him into banishment: they had plotted his assassination: they had risen against him in arms by thousands. He had avenged himself on them by havoc such as England had never before seen. Their heads and quarters were still rotting on poles in all the marketplaces of Somersetshire and Dorsetshire. Aged women, held in high honour among the sectaries for piety and charity, had, for offences which no good prince would have thought deserving even of a severe reprimand, been beheaded and burned alive. Such had been, even in England, the relations between the King and the Puritans; and in Scotland the tyranny of the King and the fury of the Puritans had been such as Englishmen could hardly conceive. To forget an enmity so long and so deadly was no light task for a nature singularly harsh and implacable.

The conflict in the royal mind did not escape the eye of Barillon.[1] At the end of January, 1687, he sent a remarkable letter to Versailles. The King, – such was the substance of this document, – had almost convinced himself that he could not obtain entire liberty for Roman Catholics and yet maintain the laws against Protestant Dissenters. He leaned, therefore, to the plan of a general indulgence; but at heart he would be far better pleased if he could, even now, divide his protection and favour between the Church of Rome and the

Church of England, to the exclusion of all other religious persuasions.

James made his first hesitating and ungracious advances towards the Puritans.

On the eighteenth of March the King informed the Privy Council that he had determined to prorogue the Parliament till the end of November, and to grant, by his own authority, entire liberty of conscience to all his subjects. On the fourth of April appeared the memorable Declaration of Indulgence. In this Declaration the King avowed that it was his earnest wish to see his people members of that Church to which he himself belonged. But, since that could not be, he announced his intention to protect them in the free exercise of their religion. He repeated all those phrases which, eight years before, when he was himself an oppressed man, had been familiar to his lips, but which he had ceased to use from the day on which a turn of fortune had put it into his power to be an oppressor. He had long been convinced, he said, that conscience was not to be forced, that persecution was unfavourable to population and to trade, and that it never attained the ends which persecutors had in view. He repeated his promise, already often repeated and often violated, that he would protect the Established Church in the enjoyment of her legal rights. He then proceeded to annul, by his own sole authority, a long series of statutes. He suspended all penal laws against all classes of Nonconformists. He authorised both Roman Catholics and Protestant Dissenters to perform their worship publicly. He forbade his subjects, on pain of his highest displeasure, to molest any religious assembly. He also abrogated all those Acts which imposed any religious test as a qualification for any civil or military office.

That the Declaration of Indulgence was unconstitutional is a point on which both the great English parties have always been entirely agreed. Every person capable of reasoning on a political question must perceive that a monarch who is competent to issue such a Declaration is nothing less than an absolute monarch.

Such, however, was the position of the parties that James's Declaration of Indulgence, though the most audacious of all the attacks made by the Stuarts on public freedom, was well calculated to please that very portion of the community by which all the other attacks of the Stuarts on public freedom had been most strenuously resisted. It could scarcely be hoped that the Protestant Nonconformist, separated from his countrymen by a harsh code harshly enforced, would be inclined to dispute the validity of a decree which relieved him from intolerable grievances. A cool and philosophical observer would undoubtedly have pronounced that all the evil arising from all the intolerant laws which Parliaments had framed was not to be compared to the evil which would be produced by a transfer of the legislative power from the Parliament to the Sovereign. But such coolness and philosophy are not to be expected from men who are smarting under present pain, and who are tempted by the offer of immediate ease. A Puritan divine might not indeed be able to deny that the dispensing power now claimed by the Crown was inconsistent with the fundamental principles of the constitution. But he might perhaps be excused if he asked, What was the constitution to him? The Act of Uniformity had ejected him, in spite of royal promises, from a benefice which was his freehold, and had reduced him to beggary and dependence. The Five Mile Act had banished him from his dwelling, from his relations, from his friends, from almost all places of public resort. Under the Conventicle Act his goods had been distrained; and he had been flung into one noisome gaol after another among highwaymen and housebreakers. Out of prison, he had constantly had the officers of justice on his track: he had been forced to pay hushmoney to informers: he had stolen, in ignominious disguises, through windows and trapdoors, to meet his flock, and had, while pouring the baptismal water, or distributing the eucharistic bread, been anxiously listening for the signal that the tipstaves were approaching. Was it not mockery to call on a man thus plundered and oppressed to suffer martyrdom for the property and liberty of his plunderers and oppressors? The Declaration, despotic as it might seem to his prosperous neighbours, brought deliverance to him. He was called upon to make his choice, not between freedom and slavery, but between two yokes; and he might not unnaturally think the yoke of the King lighter than that of the Church.

The Dissenters wavered; nor is it any reproach to them that they did so. They were suffering; and the King had given them relief. Some eminent pastors had emerged from confinement; and others had ventured to return from exile. Congregations, which had hitherto met only by stealth and in darkness, now assembled at noonday, and sung psalms aloud in the hearing of magistrates, churchwardens, and constables. Modest buildings for the worship of God after the Puritan fashion began to rise all over England. An observant traveller will still remark the date of 1687 on some of the oldest meeting houses.

That section of the dissenting body which was favourable to the King's new policy had from the first been a minority, and soon began to diminish. For the Nonconformists perceived in no long time that their spiritual privileges had been abridged rather than extended by the Indulgence. The chief characteristic of the Puritan was abhorrence of the peculiarities of the Church of Rome. He had quitted the Church of England only because he conceived that she too much resembled her superb and voluptuous sister, the sorceress of the golden cup and of the scarlet robe. He now found that one of the implied conditions of that alliance which some of his pastors had formed with the Court was that the religion of the Court should be respectfully and tenderly treated. He soon began to regret the days of persecution. While the penal laws were enforced, he had heard the words of life in secret and at his peril; but still he had heard them. When the brethren were assembled in the inner chamber, when the sentinels had been posted, when the doors had been locked, when the preacher, in the garb of a butcher or a drayman, had come in over the tiles, then at least God was truly worshipped. No portion of divine truth was suppressed or softened down for any worldly object. All the distinctive doctrines of the puritan theology were fully, and even coarsely, set forth. To the Church of Rome no quarter was given. The Beast, the Antichrist, the Man of Sin, the mystical Jezebel, the mystical Babylon, were the phrases ordinarily employed to describe that august and fascinating superstition. Such had been once the style of Alsop, of Lobb, of Rosewell, and of other ministers who had of late been well received at the palace: but such was now their style no longer. Divines who aspired to a high place in the King's favour and confidence could not venture to speak with asperity of the King's religion. Congregations therefore complained loudly that, since the appearance of the Declaration which purported to give them entire freedom of conscience, they had never once heard the Gospel boldly and faithfully preached. Formerly they had been forced to snatch their spiritual nutriment by stealth: but, when they had snatched it, they had found it seasoned exactly to their taste. They were now at liberty to feed: but their food had lost all its savour. They met by daylight, and in commodious edifices; but they heard discourses far less to their taste than they would have heard from the rector. At the parish church the will worship and idolatry of Rome were every Sunday attacked with energy: but, at the meeting house, the pastor, who had a few months before reviled the established clergy as little better than Papists, now carefully abstained from censuring Popery, or conveyed his censures in language too delicate to shock even the ears of Father Petre.[2]

On the twenty-seventh of April 1688, the King put forth a second Declaration of Indulgence. In this paper he recited at length the Declaration of the preceding April. His past life, he said, ought to have convinced his people that he was not a person who could easily be induced to depart from any resolution which he had formed. But, as designing men had attempted to persuade the world that he might be prevailed on to give way in this matter, he thought it necessary to proclaim that his purpose was immutably fixed, that he was resolved to employ those only who were prepared to concur in his design, and that he had, in pursuance of that resolution, dismissed many of his disobedient servants from civil and military employments. He announced that he meant to hold a Parliament in November at the latest; and he exhorted his subjects to choose representatives who would assist him in the great work which he had undertaken.

This Declaration at first produced little sensation. It contained nothing new; and men wondered that the King should think it worth while to publish a solemn manifesto merely for the purpose of telling them that he had not changed his mind. Perhaps James was nettled by the indifference with which the announcement of his fixed resolution was received by the public, and thought that his dignity and authority would suffer unless he without delay did something novel and striking. On the fourth of May, accordingly, he made an Order in Council that his Declaration of the preceding week should be read, on two successive Sundays, at the time of the divine service, by the officiating ministers of all the churches and chapels of the kingdom. In London and in the suburbs the reading was to take place on the twentieth and twenty-seventh of May, in other parts of England on the third and tenth of June. The Bishops were directed to distribute copies of the Declaration through their respective dioceses.

When it is considered that the clergy of the Established Church, with scarcely an exception, regarded the Indulgence as a violation of the laws of the realm, as a breach of the plighted faith of the King, and as a fatal blow levelled at the interest and dignity of their own profession, it will scarcely admit of doubt that the Order in Council was intended to be felt by them as a cruel affront. It was popularly believed that Petre had avowed this intention in a coarse metaphor borrowed from the rhetoric of the East. He would, he said, make them eat dirt, the vilest and most loathsome of all dirt. But, tyrannical and malignant as the mandate was, would the Anglican priesthood refuse to obey? The King's temper was arbitrary and severe. The proceedings of the Ecclesiastical Commission were as summary as those of a court martial. Whoever ventured to resist might in a week be ejected from his parsonage, deprived of his whole income, pronounced incapable of holding any other spiritual preferment, and left to beg from door to door. If, indeed, the whole body offered an united opposition to the royal will, it was probable that even James would scarcely venture to punish ten thousand delinquents at once. But there was not time to form an extensive combination. The Order in Council was gazetted on the seventh of May. On the twentieth the Declaration was to be read in all the pulpits of London and the neighbourhood. By no exertion was it possible in that age to ascertain within a fortnight the intentions of one tenth part of the parochial ministers who were scattered over the kingdom. It was not easy to collect in so short a time the sense even of the episcopal order. It might also well be apprehended that, if the clergy refused to read the Declaration, the Protestant Dissenters would misinterpret the refusal, would despair of obtaining any toleration from the members of the Church of England, and would throw their whole weight into the scale of the Court.

The clergy therefore hesitated; and this hesitation may well be excused: for some eminent laymen, who possessed a large share of the public confidence, were disposed to recommend submission. They thought that a general opposition could hardly be expected, and that a partial opposition would be ruinous to individuals, and of little advantage to the Church and to the nation. Such was the opinion given at this time by Halifax and Nottingham. The day drew near; and still there was no concert and no formed resolution.

At this conjuncture the Protestant Dissenters of London won for themselves a title to the lasting gratitude of their country. They had hitherto been reckoned by the government as part of its strength. A few of their most active and noisy preachers, corrupted by the favours of the Court had got up addresses in favour of the King's policy. Others, estranged by the recollection of many cruel wrongs both from the Church of England and from the House of Stuart, had seen with resentful pleasure the tyrannical prince and the tyrannical hierarchy separated by a bitter enmity, and bidding against each other for the help of sects lately persecuted and despised. But this feeling, however natural, had been indulged long enough. The time had come when it was necessary to make a choice; and the Nonconformists of the City, with a noble spirit, arrayed themselves side by side with the members of the Church in defence of the fundamental laws of the realm. Baxter, Bates, and Howe distinguished themselves by their efforts to bring about this coalition: but the generous enthusiasm which pervaded the whole Puritan body made the task easy. The zeal of the flocks outran that of the pastors. Those Presbyterian and Independent teachers who showed an inclination to take part with the King against the ecclesiastical establishment received distinct notice that, unless they changed their conduct, their congregations would neither hear them nor pay them. Alsop, who had flattered himself that he should be able to bring over a great body of his disciples to the royal side, found himself on a sudden an object of contempt and abhorrence to those who had lately revered him as their spiritual guide, sank into a deep melancholy, and hid himself from the public eye. Deputations waited on several of the

London clergy imploring them not to judge of the dissenting body from the servile adulation which had lately filled the London Gazette, and exhorting them, placed as they were in the van of this great fight, to play the men for the liberties of England and for the faith delivered to the Saints. These assurances were received with joy and gratitude. Yet there was still much anxiety and much difference of opinion among those who had to decide whether, on Sunday the twentieth, they would or would not obey the King's command.

On the eighteenth [of May] a meeting of prelates and of other eminent divines was held at Lambeth. Tillotson, Tenison, Stillingfleet, Patrick, and Sherlock were present. Prayers were solemnly read before the consultation began. After long deliberation, a petition embodying the general sense was written by the Archbishop with his own hand. It was not drawn up with much felicity of style. Indeed, the cumbrous and inelegant structure of the sentences brought on Sancroft some raillery, which he bore with less patience than he showed under much heavier trials. But in substance nothing could be more skilfully framed than this memorable document. All disloyalty, all intolerance, was earnestly disclaimed. The King was assured that the Church still was, as she had ever been, faithful to the throne. He was assured also that the Bishops would, in proper place and time, as Lords of Parliament and members of the Upper House of Convocation, show that they by no means wanted tenderness for the conscientious scruples of Dissenters. But Parliament had, both in the late and in the present reign, pronounced that the sovereign was not constitutionally competent to dispense with statutes in matters ecclesiastical. The Declaration was therefore illegal; and the petitioners could not, in prudence, honour, or conscience, be parties to the solemn publishing of an illegal Declaration in the house of God, and during the time of divine service.

This paper was signed by the Archbishop and by six of his suffragans, Lloyd of Saint Asaph, Turner of Ely, Lake of Chichester, Ken of Bath and Wells, White of Peterborough, and Trelawney of Bristol. The Bishop of London, being under suspension, did not sign.

It was now late on Friday evening; and on Sunday morning the Declaration was to be read in the churches of London. It was necessary to put the paper into the King's hands without delay. The six Bishops crossed the river to Whitehall. The Archbishop, who had long been forbidden the Court, did not accompany them. Lloyd, leaving his five brethren at the House of Lord Dartmouth in the vicinity of the palace, went to Sunderland,[3] and begged that minister to read the petition, and to ascertain when the King would be willing to receive it. Sunderland, afraid of compromising himself, refused to look at the paper, but went immediately to the royal closet. James directed that the Bishops should be admitted. He had heard from his tool Cartwright that they were disposed to obey the royal mandate, but that they wished for some little modifications in form, and that they meant to present a humble request to that effect. His Majesty was therefore in a very good humour. When they knelt before him, he graciously told them to rise, took the paper from Lloyd, and said, "This is my Lord of Canterbury's hand." "Yes, sir, his own hand," was the answer. James read the petition: he folded it up; and his countenance grew dark. "This," he said, "is a great surprise to me. I did not expect this from your Church, especially from some of you. This is a standard of rebellion." The Bishops broke out into passionate professions of loyalty: but the King, as usual, repeated the same words over and over. "I tell you, this is a standard of rebellion." "Rebellion!" cried Trelawney, falling on his knees. "For God's sake, sir, do not say so hard a thing of us. No Trelawney can be a rebel. Remember that my family has fought for the crown. Remember how I served Your Majesty when Monmouth was in the West." "We put down the last rebellion," said Lake: "we shall not raise another." "We rebel!" exclaimed Turner; "we are ready to die at your Majesty's feet." "Sir," said Ken, in a more mannerly tone, "I hope that you will grant to us that liberty of conscience which you grant to all mankind." Still James went on. "This is rebellion. This is a standard of rebellion. Did ever a good Churchman question the dispensing power before? Have not some of you preached for it and written for it? It is a standard of rebellion. I will have my Declaration published." "We have two duties to perform," answered Ken, "our duty to God, and our duty to Your Majesty. We honour you: but we fear God." "Have I deserved this?" said the King, more and more angry: "I who have been such a friend to your Church? I did not expect this from some of you. I will be obeyed. My Declaration shall be published. You are trumpeters of sedition. What do you do here? Go to your dioceses; and see that I am obeyed. I will keep this paper. I will not part with it. I will remember you that have signed it." "God's will be done," said Ken. "God has given me the dispensing power," said the King, "and I will maintain it. I tell you that there are still seven thousand of your Church who have not bowed the knee to Baal." The Bishops respectfully retired. That very evening the document which they had put into the hands of the King appeared word for word in print, was laid on the tables of all the coffeehouses, and was cried about in the streets. Everywhere the people rose from their beds, and came up to stop the hawkers. It was said that the printer cleared a thousand pounds in a few hours by this penny broadside. This is probably an exaggeration; it is an exaggeration which proves that the sale was enormous. How the petition got abroad is still a mystery.

In the City and Liberties of London were about a hundred parish churches. In only four of these was the Order in Council obeyed. At Saint Gregory's the Declaration was read by a divine of the name of Martin. As soon as he uttered the first words, the whole congregation rose and withdrew. At Saint Matthew's, in Friday Street, a wretch named Timothy Hall, who had disgraced his gown by acting as broker for the Duchess of Portsmouth in the sale of pardons, and who now had hopes of obtaining the vacant bishopric of Oxford, was in like manner left alone in his church. At Serjeant's Inn, in Chancery Lane, the clerk pretended that he had forgotten to bring a copy; and the Chief Justice of the King's Bench, who had attended in order to see that the royal mandate was obeyed, was forced to content himself with this excuse. Samuel Wesley, the father of John and Charles Wesley, a curate in London, took for his text that day the noble answer of the three Jews to the Chaldean tyrant, "Be it known unto thee, O King, that we will not serve thy gods, nor worship the golden image which thou hast set up." Even in the chapel of Saint James's Palace the officiating minister had the courage to disobey the order. The Westminster boys long remembered what took place that day in the Abbey. Sprat, Bishop of Rochester, officiated there as Dean. As soon as he began to read the Declaration, murmurs and the noise of people crowding out of the choir drowned his voice. He trembled so violently that men saw the paper shake in his hand. Long before he had finished, the place was deserted by all but those whose situation made it necessary for them to remain.

Never had the Church been so dear to the nation as on the afternoon of that day. The spirit of dissent seemed to be extinct. Baxter from his pulpit pronounced an eulogium on the Bishops and parochial clergy. The Dutch minister, a few hours later, wrote to inform the States General that the Anglican priesthood had risen in the estimation of the public to an incredible degree. The universal cry of the Nonconformists, he said, was that they would rather continue to lie under the penal statutes than separate their cause from that of the prelates.

Another week of anxiety and agitation passed away. Sunday came again. Again the churches of the capital were thronged by hundreds of thousands. The Declaration was read nowhere except at the very few places where it had been read the week before. The minister who had officiated at the chapel in Saint James's Palace had been turned out of his situation: a more obsequious divine appeared with the paper in his hand: but his agitation was so great that he could not articulate. In truth the feeling of the whole nation had now become such as none but the very best and noblest, or the very worst and basest, of mankind could without much discomposure encounter.

Even the King stood aghast for a moment at the violence of the tempest which he had raised. What step was he next to take? He must either advance or recede: and it was impossible to advance without peril, or to recede without humiliation. At one moment he determined to put forth a second order enjoining the clergy in high and angry terms to publish his Declaration, and menacing every one who should be refractory with instant suspension. This order was drawn up and sent to the press, then recalled, then a second time sent to the press, then recalled a second time. A different plan was suggested by some of those who were for rigorous measures. The prelates who had signed the petition might be cited before the Ecclesiastical Commission and deprived of their sees. But to this course strong objections were urged in Council. It had been announced that the House would be convoked before the end of the year. The Lords would assuredly treat the sentence of deprivation as a nullity, would insist that Sancroft and his fellow petitioners should be summoned to Parliament, and would refuse to acknowledge a new Archbishop of Canterbury or a new Bishop of Bath and Wells. Thus the session, which at best was likely to be sufficiently stormy, would commence with a deadly quarrel between the crown and the peers. If therefore it were thought necessary to punish the Bishops, the punishment ought to be inflicted according to the known course of English law.

Jeffreys maintained that the government would be disgraced if such transgressors as the seven Bishops were suffered to escape with a mere reprimand. He did not, however, wish them to be cited before the Ecclesiastical Commission, in which he sate as chief or rather as sole Judge. For the load of public hatred under which he already lay was too much even for his shameless forehead and obdurate heart; and he shrank from the responsibility which he would have incurred by pronouncing an illegal sentence on the rulers of the Church and the favourites of the nation. He therefore recommended a criminal information. It was accordingly resolved that the Archbishop and the six other petitioners should be brought before the Court of King's bench on a charge of seditious libel. That they would be convicted it was scarcely possible to doubt. The Judges and their officers were tools of the Court. Since the old charter of the City of London had been forfeited, scarcely one prisoner whom the government was bent on bringing to punishment had been absolved by a jury. The refractory prelates would probably be condemned to ruinous fines and to long imprisonment, and would be glad to ransom themselves by serving, both in and out of Parliament, the designs of the Sovereign.

On the twenty-seventh of May it was notified to the Bishops that on the eighth of June they must appear before the King in Council. Why so long an interval was allowed we are not informed. Perhaps James hoped that some of the offenders, terrified by his displeasure, might submit before the day fixed for the reading of the Declaration in their dioceses, and might, in order to make their peace with him, persuade their clergy to obey his order. If such was his hope it was signally disappointed. Sunday the third of June came; and in all parts of England followed the example of the capital. Already the Bishops of Norwich, Gloucester, Salisbury, Winchester, and Exeter had signed copies of the petition in token of their approbation. The Bishop of Worcester had refused to distribute the Declaration among his clergy. The Bishop of Hereford had distributed it: but it was generally understood that he was overwhelmed by remorse and shame for having done so. Not one parish priest in fifty complied with the Order in Council. In the great diocese of Chester, including the county of Lancaster, only three clergymen could be prevailed on by Cartwright to obey the King. In the diocese of Norwich are many hundreds of parishes. In only four of these was the Declaration read. The courtly Bishop of Rochester could not overcome the scruples of the minister of the ordinary of Chatham, who depended on the government for bread. There is still extant a pathetic letter which this honest priest sent to the Secretary of the Admiralty. "I cannot," he wrote, "reasonably expect Your Honour's protection. God's will be done. I must choose suffering rather than sin."

On the evening of the eighth of June the seven prelates, furnished by the ablest lawyers in England with full advice, repaired to the palace and were called into the Council chamber. Their petition was lying on the table. The Chancellor took the paper up, showed it to the Archbishop, and said, "Is this the paper which your Grace wrote, and which the six Bishops present delivered to His Majesty?" Sancroft looked at the paper, turned to the King, and spoke thus: "Sir, I stand here a culprit. I never was so before. Once I little thought that I ever should be so. Least of all could I think that I should be charged with any offence against my King: but, since I am so unhappy as to be in this situation, Your Majesty will not be offended if I avail myself of my lawful right to decline saying anything which may incriminate me." "This is mere chicanery," said the King. "I hope that Your Grace will not do so ill a thing as to deny your own hand." "Sir," said Lloyd, whose studies had been much among the casuists, "all divines agree that a person situated as we are may refuse to answer such a question."

The King was so absurd as to think himself personally affronted because they chose, on a legal question, to be guided by legal advice. "You believe every body," he said, "rather than me." He was indeed mortified and alarmed. For he had gone so far that, if they persisted, he had no choice left but to send them to prison; and though he by no means foresaw all the consequences of such a step, he foresaw probably enough to disturb him. They were resolute. A warrant was therefore made out directing the Lieutenant of the Tower to keep them in safe custody, and a large barge was manned to convey them down the river.

It was known all over London that the Bishops were before the Council. The public anxiety was intense. A great multitude filled the courts of Whitehall and all the neighbouring streets. Many people were in the habit of refreshing themselves at the close of a summer day with the cool air of the Thames. But on this evening the whole river was alive with wherries. When the Seven came forth under a guard, the emotions of the people broke through all restraint. Thousands fell on their knees and prayed aloud for the men who had, with the Christian courage of Ridley and Latimer, confronted a tyrant inflamed by all the bigotry of Mary. Many dashed into the stream, and, up to their waists in ooze and water, cried to the holy fathers to bless them. All down the river, from Whitehall to London Bridge, the royal barge passed between lines of boats, from which arose a shout of "God bless your Lordships." The King, in great alarm, gave orders that the garrison of the Tower should be doubled, that the Guards should be held ready for action, and that two companies should be detached from every regiment in the kingdom, and sent up instantly to London. But the force on which he relied as the means of coercing the people shared all the feelings of the people. The very sentinels who were posted at the Traitors' Gate reverently asked for a blessing from the martyrs whom they were to guard. Sir Edward Hales was Lieutenant of the Tower. He was little inclined to treat his prisoners with kindness. For he was an apostate from that Church for which they suffered; and he held several lucrative posts by virtue of that dispensing power against which they had protested. He learned with indignation that his soldiers were drinking to the health of the Bishops. He ordered his officers to see that it was done no more. But the officers came back with a report that the thing could not be prevented, and that no other health was drunk in the garrison. Nor was it only by carousing that the troops showed their reverence for the fathers of the Church. There was such a show of devotion throughout the Tower that pious men thanked God for bringing good out of evil, and for making the persecution of His faithful servants the means of saving many souls. All day the coaches and liveries of the first nobles of England were seen round the prison gates. Thousands of humbler spectators constantly covered Tower Hill. But among the marks of public respect and sympathy which the prelates received there was one which more than all the rest enraged and alarmed the King. He learned that a deputation of ten Nonconformist ministers had visited the Tower. He sent for four of these persons, and himself upbraided them. They courageously answered that they thought it their duty to forget past quarrels, and to stand by the men who stood by the Protestant religion.

Scarcely had the gates of the Tower been closed on the prisoners when an event took place which increased the public excitement. It had been announced that the Queen did not expect to be confined till July. But, on the day after the Bishops had appeared before the Council, it was observed that the King seemed to be anxious about her state. In the evening, however, she sate playing cards at Whitehall till near midnight. Then she was carried in a sedan to Saint James's Palace, where apartments had been very hastily fitted up for her reception. Soon messengers were running about in all directions to summon physicians and priests, Lords of the Council, and Ladies of the Bedchamber. In a few hours many public functionaries and women of rank were assembled in the Queen's room. There, on the morning of Sunday, the tenth of June, a day long kept sacred by the too faithful adherents of a bad cause, was born the most unfortunate of princes, destined to twenty-seven years of exile and wandering, of vain projects, of honours more galling than insults, and of hopes such as make the heart sick.

The calamities of the poor child had begun before his birth. The nation over which, according to the ordinary course of succession, he would have reigned was fully persuaded that his mother was not really pregnant. By whatever evidence the fact of his birth had been proved, a considerable number of people would probably have persisted in maintaining that the Jesuits had practised some skilful sleight of hand; and the evidence, partly from accident, partly from gross mismanagement, was really open to some objections. Many persons of both sexes were in the royal bedchamber when the child first saw the light; but none of them enjoyed any large measure of public confidence. Of the Privy Councillors present, half were Roman Catholics; and those who called themselves Protestants were generally regarded as traitors to their country and their God. Many of the women in attendance were French, Italian, and Portuguese. Of the

English ladies some were Papists, and some were the wives of Papists. Some persons who were peculiarly entitled to be present, and whose testimony would have satisfied all minds accessible to reason, were absent; and for their absence the King was held responsible. The Princess Anne was, of all inhabitants of the island, the most deeply interested in the event. Her sex and her experience qualified her to act as the guardian of her sister's birthright and her own. She had conceived strong suspicions, which were daily confirmed by circumstances trifling or imaginary. She fancied that the Queen carefully shunned her scrutiny, and ascribed to guilt a reserve which was perhaps the effect of delicacy. In this temper Anne had determined to be present and vigilant when the critical day should arrive. But she had not thought it necessary to be at her post a month before that day, and had, in compliance, it was said, with her father's advice, gone to drink the Bath waters. Sancroft, whose great place made it his duty to attend, and on whose probity the nation placed entire reliance, had a few hours before been sent to the Tower by James. The Hydes[4] were the proper protectors of the rights of the two Princesses. The Dutch Ambassador might be regarded as the representative of William, who, as first prince of the blood and consort of the King's eldest daughter, had a deep interest in what was passing. James never thought of summoning any member, male or female, of the family of Hyde; nor was the Dutch Ambassador to be present.

Posterity has fully acquitted the King of the fraud which his people imputed to him. But it is impossible to acquit him of folly and perverseness such as explain and excuse the error of his contemporaries. He was perfectly aware of the suspicions which were abroad. He ought to have known that those suspicions would not be dispelled by the evidence of members of the Church of Rome, or of persons who, though they might call themselves members of the Church of England, had shown themselves ready to sacrifice the interests of the Church of England in order to obtain his favour. That he was taken by surprise is true. But he had twelve hours to make his arrangements. He found no difficulty in crowding St. James's Palace with bigots and sycophants on whose word the nation placed no reliance. It would have been quite as easy to procure the attendance of some eminent persons whose attachment to the Princesses and to the established religion was unquestionable.

The cry of the whole nation was that an imposture had been practised. Papists had, during some months, been predicting, from the pulpit and through the press, in pose and verse, in English and Latin, that a Prince of Wales would be given to the prayers of the Church; and they had now accomplished their own prophecy. Every witness who could not be corrupted or deceived had been studiously excluded. Anne had been tricked into visiting Bath. The Primate had, on the very day preceding that which had been fixed for the villany, been sent to prison in defiance of the rules of law and of the privileges of peerage. Not a single man or woman who had the smallest interest in detecting the fraud had been suffered to be present. The Queen had been removed suddenly and at the dead of night to Saint James's Palace, because that building, less commodious for honest purposes than Whitehall, had some rooms and passages well suited for the purpose of the Jesuits. There, amidst a circle of zealots who thought nothing a crime that tended to promote the interests of their Church, and of courtiers who thought nothing a crime that tended to enrich and aggrandise themselves, a new born child had been introduced, by means of a warming pan, into the royal bed, and then handed round in triumph, as heir of three kingdoms. Heated by such suspicions, suspicions unjust, it is true, but not altogether unnatural, men thronged more eagerly than ever to pay their homage to the saintly victims of the tyrant, who, having long foully injured his people, had now filled up the measure of his iniquities by more foully injuring his children.

The Prince of Orange, not himself suspecting any trick, and not aware of the state of public feeling in England, ordered prayers to be said under his own roof for his little brother in law, and sent Zulestein to London with a formal message of congratulation. Zulestein, to his amazement, found all the people whom he met open mouthed about the infamous fraud just committed by the Jesuits, and saw every hour some fresh pasquinade on the pregnancy and the delivery. He soon wrote to the Hague that not one person in ten believed the child to have been born of the Queen.

The demeanour of the seven prelates meanwhile strengthened the interest which their situation excited. On the evening of the Black Friday, as it was called, on which they were committed, they reached their prison just at the hour of divine service. They instantly hastened to the chapel. It chanced that in the second lesson were these words: "In all things approving ourselves as the ministers of God, in much patience, in afflictions, in distresses, in stripes, in imprisonments." All zealous Churchmen were delighted by this coincidence, and remembered how much comfort a similar coincidence had given, near forty years before, to Charles the First at the time of his death.

The Bishops edified all who approached them by the firmness and cheerfulness with which they endured confinement, by the modesty and meekness with which they received the applauses and blessings of the whole nation, and by the loyal attachment which they professed for the persecutor who sought their destruction. They remained only a week in custody. On Friday, the fifteenth of June, the first day of term, they were brought before the King's Bench. An immense throng awaited their coming. From the landing-place to the Court of Requests they passed through a lane of spectators who blessed and applauded them. "Friends," said the prisoners as they passed, "honour the King; and remember us in your prayers." These humble and pious expressions moved the hearers even to tears. When at length the procession had made its way through the crowd into the presence of the Judges, the Attorney General exhibited the information which he had been commanded to prepare, and moved that the defendants might be ordered to plead. The counsel on the other side objected that the Bishops had been unlawfully committed, and were therefore not regularly before the Court. The question whether a peer could be required to enter into recognisances on a charge of libel was argued at great length, and decided by a majority of the Judges in favour of the crown. The prisoners then pleaded Not Guilty. That day fortnight, the twenty-ninth of June, was fixed for their trial. In the meantime they were allowed to be at large on their own recognisances. The crown lawyers acted prudently in not requiring sureties. For Halifax had arrange that twenty-one temporal peers of the highest consideration should be ready to put in bail, three for each defendant; and such a manifestation of the feeling of the nobility would have been no slight blow to the government. It was also known that one of the most opulent Dissenters of the City had begged that he might have the honour of giving security for Ken.

The Bishops were now permitted to depart to their own homes. The common people, who did not understand the nature of the legal proceedings which had taken place in the King's Bench, and who saw that their favourites had been brought to Westminster Hall in custody and were suffered to go away in freedom, imagined that the good cause was prospering. Loud acclamations were raised. The steeples of the Churches sent forth joyous peals. Sprat[5] was amazed to hear the bells of his own Abbey ringing merrily. He promptly silenced them; but his interference caused much angry muttering. The Bishops found it difficult to escape from the importunate crowd of their wellwishers. Lloyd was detained in Palace Yard by admirers who struggled to touch his hands and to kiss the skirt of his robe, till Clarendon, with some difficulty, rescued him and conveyed him home by a bypath. Cartwright, it is said, was so unwise as to mingle with the crowd. A person who saw his Episcopal habit asked and received his blessing. A bystander cried out, "Do you know who blessed you?" "Surely," said he who had just been honoured by the benediction, "it was one of the Seven." "No," said the other, "it is the Popish Bishop of Chester." "Popish dog," cried the enraged Protestant: "take your blessing back again."

Such was the concourse, and such the agitation, that the Dutch Ambassador was surprised to see the day close without an insurrection. The King had been anxious and irritable. In order that he might be ready to suppress any disturbance, he had passed the morning in reviewing several battalions of infantry in Hyde Park. It is, however, by no means certain that his troops would have stood by him if he had needed their services. When Sancroft reached Lambeth, in the afternoon, he found the footguards, who were quartered in that suburb, assembled before the gate of his palace. They formed in two lines on his right and left, and asked his benediction as he went through them. He with difficulty prevented them from lighting a bonfire in honour of his return to his dwelling. There were, however, many bonfires that evening in the City. Two Roman Catholics, who were so indiscreet as to beat some boys for joining in these rejoicings, were seized by the mob, stripped naked, and ignominiously branded.

Sir Edward Hales now came to demand fees from those who had lately been his prisoners. They refused to pay anything for a detention which they regarded as illegal to an officer whose commission was, on their principles, a nullity. The Lieutenant hinted very intelligibly that, if they came into his hands again, they should be put into heavy irons and should lie on bare stones. "We are under our King's displeasure," was the answer; "and most deeply do we feel it: but a fellow subject who threatens us does but lose his breath." It is easy to imagine with what indignation the people, excited as they were, must have learned that a renegade from the Protestant faith, who held a command in defiance of the fundamental laws of England, had dared to menace divines of venerable age and dignity with all the barbarities of Lollard's Tower.

Before the day of trial the agitation had spread to the farthest corners of the island. From Scotland the Bishops received letters assuring them of the sympathy of the

Presbyterians of that country, so long and so bitterly hostile to prelacy. The people of Cornwall, a fierce, bold, and athletic race, among whom there was a stronger provincial feeling than in any other part of the realm, were greatly moved by the danger of Trelawney, whom they reverenced less as a ruler of the Church than as the head of an honourable house, and the heir through twenty descents of ancestors who had been of great note before the Normans had set foot on English ground. All over the country the peasants chanted a ballad of which the burden is still remembered:

"And shall Trelawney die, and shall Trelawney die? Then thirty thousand Cornish boys will know the reason why."

The miners from their caverns reechoed the song with a variation:

"Then twenty thousand under ground will know the reason why."

The rustics in many parts of the country loudly expressed as strange hope which had never ceased to live in their hearts. Their Protestant Duke, their beloved Monmouth, would suddenly appear, would lead them to victory, and would tread down the King and the Jesuits under his feet.

The ministers were appalled. Even Jeffreys would gladly have retraced his steps. He charged Clarendon with friendly messages to the Bishops, and threw on others the blame of the prosecution which he had himself recommended. Sunderland again ventured to recommend concession.

The late auspicious birth, he said, had given the King an excellent opportunity of withdrawing from a position full of danger and inconvenience without incurring the reproach of timidity or of caprice. On such happy occasions it had been usual for sovereigns to make the hearts of subjects glad by acts of clemency; and nothing could be more advantageous to the Prince of Wales than that he should, while still in his cradle, be the peacemaker between his father and the agitated nation. But the King's resolution was fixed. "I will go on," he said. "I have been only too indulgent. Indulgence ruined my father." The artful minister found that his advice had been formerly taken only because it had been shaped to suit the royal temper, and that, from the moment at which he began to counsel well, he began to counsel in vain.

To pack a jury now was the great object of the King. The crown lawyers were ordered to make strict enquiry as to the sentiments of the persons who were registered in the freeholders' book. Sir Samuel Astry, Clerk of the Crown, whose duty it was, in cases of this description, to select the names, was summoned to the palace, and had an interview with James in the presence of the Chancellor. Sir Samuel seems to have done his best. For, among the forty-eight persons whom he nominated, were said to be several servants of the King, and several Roman Catholics. But as the counsel for the Bishops had a right to strike off twelve, these persons were removed. The crown lawyers also struck off twelve. The list was thus reduced to twenty-four. The first twelve who answered to their names were to try the issue.

On the twenty-ninth of June, Westminster Hall, Old and New Palace Yard, and all the neighbouring streets to a great distance were thronged with people. Such an auditory had never before and has never since been assembled in the Court of King's Bench. Thirty-five temporal peers of the realm were counted in the crowd.

All the four Judges of the Court were on the bench. Wright, who presided, had been raised to his high place over the heads of many abler and more learned men solely on account of his unscrupulous servility. Allibone was a Papist, and owed his situation to that dispensing power, the legality of which was now in question. Holloway had hitherto been a serviceable tool of the government. Even Powell, whose character for honesty stood high, had borne a part in some proceedings which it is impossible to defend. He had, in the great case of Sir Edward Hales, with some hesitation, it is true, and after some delay, concurred with the majority of the bench, and had thus brought on his character a stain which his honourable conduct on this day completely effaced.

The counsel were by no means fairly matched. The government had required from its law officers services so odious and disgraceful that all the ablest jurists and advocates of the Tory party had, one after another, refused to comply, and had been dismissed from their employments. Sir Thomas Powis, the Attorney General, was scarcely of the third rank in his profession. Sir William Williams, the Solicitor General, had great abilities and dauntless courage: but he wanted discretion; he loved wrangling; he had no command over his temper; and he was hated and despised by all political parties. The most conspicuous assistants of the Attorney and Solicitor were Serjeant Trinder, a Roman Catholic, and Sir Bartholomew Shower, Recorder of London, who had some legal learning, but whose fulsome apologies and endless repetitions were the jest of Westminster Hall.

The government had wished to secure the services of Maynard: but he had plainly declared that he could not in conscience do what was asked of him.

On the other side were arrayed almost all the eminent forensic talents of the age. Sawyer and Finch, who, at the time of the accession of James, had been Attorney and Solicitor General, and who, during the persecution of the Whigs in the late reign, had served the crown with but too much vehemence and success, were of counsel for the defendants. With them were joined two person who, since age had diminished the activity of Maynard, were reputed the two best lawyers that could be found in the Inns of Court; Pemberton, who had, in the time of Charles the Second, been Chief Justice of the King's Bench, who had been removed from his high place on account of his humanity and moderation, and who had resumed his practice at the bar; and Pollexfen, who had long been at the head of the Western circuit, and who, though he had incurred much unpopularity by holding briefs for the crown at the Bloody Assizes, and particularly by appearing against Alice Lisle, was known to be at heart a Whig, if not a republican. Sir Creswell Levinz was also there, a man of great knowledge and experience, but of singularly timid nature. He had been removed from the bench some years before, because he was afraid to serve the purposes of the government. He was now afraid to appear as the advocate of the Bishops, and had at first refused to receive their retainer: but it was intimated to him by the whole body of attorneys who employed him that, if he declined this brief, he should never have another.

Sir George Treby, an able and zealous Whig, who had been Recorder of London under the old charter, was on the same side. Sir John Holt, a still more eminent Whig lawyer, was not retained for the defence, in consequence, it should seem, of some prejudice conceived against him by Sancroft, but was privately consulted on the case by the Bishop of London. The junior counsel for the Bishops was a young barrister named John Somers. He had no advantages of birth or fortune; nor had he yet had the opportunity of distinguishing himself before the eyes of the public: but his genius, his industry, his great and various accomplishments, were well known to a small circle of friends; and, in spite of his Whig opinions, his pertinent and lucid mode of arguing and the constant propriety of his demeanour had already secured to him the ear of the Court of King's Bench. The importance of obtaining his services had been strongly represented to the Bishops by Johnstone; and Pollexfen, it is said, had declared that no man in Westminster Hall was so well qualified to treat a historical and constitutional question as Somers.

The jury was sworn. It consisted of persons of highly respectable station. The foreman was Sir Roger Langley, a baronet of old and honourable family. With him were joined a knight and ten esquires, several of whom are known to have been men of large possessions. There were some Nonconformists in that number: for the Bishops were wisely resolved not to show any distrust of the Protestant Dissenters. One name excited considerable alarm, that of Michael Arnold. He was brewer to the palace; and it was apprehended that the government counted on his voice. The story goes that he complained bitterly of the position in which he found himself. "Whatever I do," he said, "I am sure to be half ruined. If I say Not Guilty, I shall brew no more for the King; and if I say Guilty, I shall brew no more for anybody else."

The trial then commenced, a trial which, even when coolly perused after the lapse of more than a century and a half, has all the interest of a drama. The advocates contended on both sides with far more than professional keenness and vehemence; the audience listened with as much anxiety as if the fate of every one of them was to be decided by the verdict; and the turns of fortune were so sudden and amazing that the multitude repeatedly passed in a single minute from anxiety to exultation, and back again from exultation to still deeper anxiety.

The information charged the Bishops with having written or published, in the county of Middlesex, a false, malicious, and seditious libel. The Attorney and Solicitor first tried to prove the writing. For this purpose several persons were called to speak to the hands of the Bishops. But the witnesses were so unwilling that hardly a single plain answer could be extracted from any of them. Pemberton, Pollexfen, and Levinz contended that there was evidence to go to the jury. Two of the Judges, Holloway and Powell, declared themselves of the same opinion; and the hopes of the spectators rose high. All at once the crown lawyers announced their intention to take another line. Powis, with shame and reluctance which he could not dissemble, put into the witness box Blathwayt, a Clerk of the Privy Council, who had been present when the King interrogated the Bishops. Blathwayt swore that he had heard them own their signatures. His testimony was decisive. "Why," said Judge Holloway to the Attorney, "when you had such evidence, did you not produce it at first, without all this waste of time?" It soon appeared why the counsel for the crown had been unwilling, without absolute necessity, to resort to this mode of proof. Pemberton stopped Blathwayt, subjected him to a searching cross examination, and insisted upon having all that had passed between the King and the defendants fully related. "That is a pretty thing indeed," cried Williams. "Do you think," said Powis, "that you are at liberty to ask our witnesses any impertinent question that comes into your heads?" The advocates of the Bishops were not men to be so put down. "He is sworn," said Pollexfen, "to tell the truth and the whole truth; and an answer we must and will have." The witness shuffled, equivocated, pretended to misunderstand the questions, implored the protection of the Court. But he was in hands from which it was not easy to escape. At length the Attorney again interposed. "If," he said, "you persist in asking such a question, tell us, at least, what use you mean to make of it." Pemberton, who, through the whole trial, did his duty manfully and ably, replied without hesitation: "My Lords, I will answer Mr. Attorney. I will deal plainly with the Court. If the Bishops owned this paper under a promise from His Majesty that their confession should not be used against them, I hope that no unfair advantage will be taken of them." "You put on His Majesty what I dare hardly name," said Williams. "Since you will be so pressing, I demand, for the King, that the question may be recorded." "What do you mean, Mr. Solicitor?" said Sawyer, interposing. "I know what I mean," said the apostate: "I desire that the question may be recorded in court." "Record what you will. I am not afraid of you, Mr. Solicitor," said Pemberton. Then came a loud and fierce altercation, which Wright could with difficulty quiet. In other circumstances, he would probably have ordered the question to be recorded, and Pemberton to be committed. But on this great day the unjust judge was overawed. He often cast as side glance towards the thick rows of Earls and Barons by whom he was watched, and before whom, in the next Parliament, he might stand at the bar. He looked, a bystander said, as if all the peers present had halters in their pockets. At length Blathwayt was forced to give a full account of what had passed. It appeared that the King had entered into no express covenant with the Bishops. But it appeared also that the Bishops might not unreasonably think that there was an implied engagement. Indeed, from the unwillingness of the crown lawyers to put the Clerk of the Council into the witness box, and from the vehemence with which they objected to Pemberton's cross examination, it is plain that they were themselves of this opinion.

However, the handwriting was now proved. But a new and serious objection was raised. It was not sufficient to prove that the Bishops had written the alleged libel. It was necessary to prove also that they had written it in the county of Middlesex. And not only was it out of the power of the Attorney and Solicitor to prove this; but it was in the power of the defendants to prove the contrary. For it so happened that Sancroft had never once left the palace at Lambeth from the time when the Order in Council appeared till after the petition was in the King's hands. The whole case for the prosecution had therefore completely broken down; and the audience, with great glee, expected a speedy acquittal.

The crown lawyers then changed their ground again, abandoned altogether the charge of writing a libel, and undertook to prove that the Bishops had published a libel in the county of Middlesex. The difficulties were great. The delivery of the petition to the King was undoubtedly, in the eye of the law, a publication. But how was this delivery to be proved? No person had been present at the audience in the royal closet except the King and the defendants. The King could not well be sworn. It was therefore only by the admissions of the defendants that the fact of publication could be established. Blathwayt was again examined, but in vain. He well remembered, he said, that the Bishops owned their hands; but he did not remember that they owned the paper which lay on the table of the Privy Council to be the same paper which they had delivered to the king, or that they were even interrogated on that point. Several other official men who had been in attendance on the Council were called, and among them Samuel Pepys, Secretary of the Admiralty, but none of them could remember that anything was said about the delivery. It was to no purpose that Williams put leading questions till the counsel on the other side declared that such twisting, such wiredrawing, was never seen in a court of justice, and till Wright himself was forced to admit that the Solicitor's mode of examination was contrary to all rule. As witness after witness answered in the negative, roars of laughter and shouts of triumph, which the Judges did not even attempt to silence, shook the hall.

It seemed that at length this hard fight had been won. The case for the crown was closed. Had the counsel for the Bishops remained silent, an acquittal was certain; for nothing which the most corrupt and shameless Judge could venture to call legal evidence of publication had been given. The Chief Justice was beginning to charge the jury, and would undoubtedly have directed them to acquit the defendants; but Finch, too anxious to be perfectly discreet, interfered, and begged to be heard. "If you will be heard," said Wright, "you shall be heard; but you do not understand your own interests." The other counsel for the defence made Finch sit down, and begged the Chief Justice to proceed. He was about to do so, when a messenger came to the Solicitor General with news that Lord Sunderland could prove the publication, and would come down to the court immediately. Wright maliciously told the counsel for the defence that they only had themselves to thank for the turn which things had taken. The countenances of the great multitude fell. Finch was, during some hours, the most unpopular man in the country. Why could he not sit still as his betters, Sawyer, Pemberton, and Pollexfen, had done? His love of meddling, his ambition to make a fine speech, had ruined everything.

Meanwhile the Lord President was brought in a sedan chair through the hall. Not a hat moved as he passed; and many voices cried out "Popish dog." He came into court pale and trembling, with eyes fixed on the ground, and gave his evidence in a faltering voice. He swore that the Bishops had informed him of their intention to present a petition to the King, and that they had been admitted into the royal closet for that purpose. This circumstance, coupled with the circumstance that, after they left the closet, there was in the King's hands a petition signed by them, was such proof as might reasonably satisfy a jury on the fact of the publication.

Publication in Middlesex was then proved. But was the paper thus published a false, malicious, and seditious libel? Hitherto the matter in dispute had been whether a fact which every body well knew to be true could be proved according to technical rules of evidence; but now the contest became one of deeper interest. It was necessary to enquire into the limits of prerogative and liberty, into the right of the King to dispense with statutes, into the right of the subject to petition for the redress of grievances. During three hours the counsel for the petitioners argued with great force in defence of the fundamental principles of the constitution, and proved from the Journals of the House of Commons that the Bishops had affirmed no more than the truth when they represented to the King that the dispensing power which he claimed had been repeatedly declared illegal by Parliament. Somers rose last. He spoke little more than five minutes: but every word was full of weighty matter; and when he sate down his reputation as an orator and a constitutional lawyer was established. He went through the expressions which were used in the information to describe the offence imputed to the Bishops, and showed that every word, whether adjective or substantive, was altogether inappropriate. The offence imputed was a false, a malicious, a seditious libel. False the paper was not; for every fact which it set forth had been shown from the journals of Parliament to be true. Malicious the paper was not; for the defendants had not sought an occasion of strife, but had been placed by the government in such a situation that they must either oppose themselves to the royal will, or violate the most sacred obligations of conscience and honour. Seditious the paper was not; for it had not been scattered by the writers among the rabble, but delivered privately into the hands of the King alone; and a libel it was not, but a decent petition such as, by the laws of England, nay by the laws of imperial Rome, by the laws of all civilised states, a subject who thinks himself aggrieved may with propriety present to the sovereign.

The Attorney replied shortly and feebly. The Solicitor spoke at great length and with great acrimony, and was often interrupted by the clamours and hisses of the audience. He went so far as to lay it down that no subject or body of subjects, except the Houses of Parliament, had a right to petition the King. The galleries were furious; and the Chief Justice himself stood aghast at the effrontery of this venal turncoat.

At length Wright proceeded to sum up the evidence. His language showed that the awe in which he stood of the government was tempered by the awe with which the audience, so numerous, so splendid, and so strongly excited, had impressed him. He said that he would give no opinion on the question of the dispensing power; that it was not necessary for him to do so; that he could not agree with much of the Solicitor's speech; that it was the right of the subject to petition; but that the particular petition before the Court was improperly worded, and was, in the contemplation of law, a libel. Allibone was of the same mind, but, in giving his opinion, showed such gross ignorance of law and history as brought on him the contempt of all who heard him. Holloway evaded the question of the dispensing power, but said that the petition seemed to him to be such as subjects who think themselves aggrieved are entitled to present, and therefore no libel. Powell took a bolder course. He avowed that, in his judgement, the Declaration of Indulgence was a nullity, and that the dispensing power, as lately exercised, was utterly inconsistent with all law. If these encroachments of prerogative were allowed, there was an end of Parliaments. The whole legislative authority would be in the King. "That issue, gentlemen," he said, "I leave to God and to your consciences."

It was dark before the jury retired to consider of their verdict. The night was a night of intense anxiety. Some letters are extant which were despatched during that period of suspense, and which have therefore an interest of a peculiar kind. "It is very late," wrote the Papal Nuncio, "and the decision is not yet known. The judges and the culprits have gone to their own homes. The jury remain together. Tomorrow we shall learn the event of this great struggle."

The solicitor for the Bishops sate up all night with a body of servants on the stairs leading to the room where the jury was consulting. It was absolutely necessary to watch the officers who watched the doors; for those officers were supposed to be in the interest of the crown, and might, it not carefully observed, have furnished a courtly juryman with food, which would have enabled him to starve out the other eleven. Strict guard was therefore kept. Not even a candle to light a pipe was permitted to enter. Some basins of water for washing were suffered to pass at about four in the morning, The jurymen, raging with thirst, soon lapped up the whole. Great numbers of people walked the neighbouring streets till dawn. Every hour a messenger came from Whitehall to know what was passing. Voices, high in altercation, were repeatedly heard within the room: but nothing certain was known.

At first nine were for acquitting and three for convicting. Two of the minority soon gave way: but Arnold was obstinate. Thomas Austin, a country gentleman of great estate, who had paid close attention to the evidence and speeches, and had taken full notes, wished to argue the question. Arnold declined. He was not used, he doggedly said, to reasoning and debating. His conscience was not satisfied; and he should not acquit the Bishops. "If you come to that," said Austin, "look at me. I am the largest and strongest of the twelve; and before I find such a petition as this a libel, here

I will stay till I am no bigger than a tobacco pipe." It was six in the morning before Arnold yielded. It was soon known that the jury were agreed: but what the verdict would be was still a secret.

At ten the Court again met. The crowd was greater than ever. The jury appeared in the box; and there was a breathless stillness.

Sir Samuel Astry spoke. "Do you find the defendants, or any of them, guilty of the misdemeanour whereof they are impeached, or not guilty?" Sir Roger Langley answered, "Not Guilty." As the words were uttered, Halifax sprang up and waved his hat. At that signal, benches and galleries raised a shout. In a moment ten thousand persons, who crowded the great hall, replied with a still louder shout, which made the old oaken roof crack; and in another moment the innumerable throng without set up a third huzza, which was heard at Temple Bar. The boats which covered the Thames gave an answering cheer. A peal of gunpowder was heard on the water, and another, and another; and so in a few moments, the glad tidings went flying past the Savoy and the Friars to London Bridge, and to the forest of masts below. As the news spread, streets and squares, marketplaces and coffeehouses, broke forth into acclamations. Yet were the acclamations less strange than the weeping. For the feelings of men had been wound up to such a point that at length the stern English nature, so little used to outward signs of emotion, gave way, and thousands sobbed aloud for very joy. Meanwhile, from the outskirts of the multitude, horsemen were spurring off to bear along all the great roads intelligence of the victory of our Church and nation. Yet not even that astounding explosion could awe the bitter and intrepid spirit of the Solicitor. Striving to make himself heard above the din, he called on the Judges to commit those who had violated, by clamour, the dignity of a court of justice. One of the rejoicing populace was seized. But the tribunal felt that it would be absurd to punish a single individual for an offence common to hundreds of thousands, and dismissed him with a gentle reprimand.

It was vain to think of passing at that moment to any other business. Indeed the roar of the multitude was such that, during half an hour, scarcely a word could be heard in the court. Williams got to his coach amidst a tempest of hisses and curses. Cartwright, whose curiosity was ungovernable, had been guilty of the folly and indecency of coming to Westminster in order to hear the decision. He was recognised by his sacerdotal garb and by his corpulent figure, and was hooted through the hall. "Take care," said one, "of the wolf in sheep's clothing." "Make room," cried another, "for the man with the Pope in his belly."

The acquitted prelates took refuge in the nearest chapel from the crowd which implored their blessing. Many churches were open on that morning throughout the capital; and many pious persons repaired thither. The bells of all the parishes of the City and liberties were ringing. The jury meanwhile could scarcely make their way out of the hall. They were forced to shake hands with hundreds. "God bless you!" cried the people; "God prosper your families! you have done like honest goodnatured gentlemen: you have saved us all to-day." As the noblemen who had attended to support the good cause drove off, they flung from their carriage windows handfuls of money, and bade the crowd drink to the health of the King, the Bishops, and the jury.

The Attorney went with the tidings to Sunderland, who happened to be conversing with the Nuncio. "Never," said Powis, "within man's memory, have there been such shouts and such tears of joy as today." The King had that morning visited the camp on Hounslow Heath. Sunderland instantly sent a courier thither with the news. James was in Lord Feversham's tent when the express arrived. He was greatly disturbed, and exclaimed in French, "So much the worse for them." He soon set out for London. While he was present, respect prevented the soldiers from giving a loose to their feelings; but he had scarcely quitted the camp when he heard a great shouting behind him. He was surprised, and asked what that uproar meant. "Nothing," was the answer: "the soldiers are glad that the Bishops are acquitted." "Do you call that nothing?" said James. And then he repeated, "So much the worse for them."

He might well be out of temper. His defeat had been complete and most humiliating. Had the prelates escaped on account of some technical defect in the case for the crown, had they escaped because they had not written the petition in Middlesex, or because it was impossible to prove, according to the strict rules of law, that they had delivered to the King the paper for which they were called in question, the prerogative would have suffered no shock. Happily for the country, the fact of publication had been fully established. The counsel for the defence had therefore been forced to attack the dispensing power. They had attacked it with great learning, eloquence and boldness. The advocates of the government had been by universal acknowledgement overmatched in the contest. Not a single Judge had ventured to declare that the Declaration of Indulgence was legal. One

Judge had in the strongest terms pronounced it illegal. The language of the whole town was that the dispensing power had received a fatal blow. Finch, who had the day before been universally reviled, was now universally applauded. He had been unwilling, it was said, to let the case be decided in a way which would have left the great constitutional question still doubtful. He had felt that a verdict which should acquit his clients, without condemning the Declaration of Indulgence, would be but half a victory. It is certain that Finch deserved neither the reproaches which had been cast on him while the event was doubtful, nor the praises which he received when it had proved happy. It was absurd to blame him because, during the short delay which he occasioned, the crown lawyers unexpectedly discovered new evidence. It was equally absurd to suppose that he deliberately exposed his clients to risk in order to establish a general principle; and still more absurd was it to praise him for what would have been a gross violation of professional duty.

That joyful day was followed by a not less joyful evening. The Bishops, and some of their most respectable friends, in vain exerted themselves to prevent tumultuous demonstrations of public feeling. Never within the memory of the oldest, not even on that night on which it was known through London that the army of Scotland had declared for a free Parliament, had the streets been in such a glare with bonfires. Round every bonfire crowds were drinking good health to the Bishops and confusion to the Papists. The windows were lighted with rows of candles. Each row consisted of seven; and the taper in the centre, which was taller than the rest, represented the Primate. The noise of rockets, squibs, and firearms, was incessant. One huge pile of faggots blazed right in front of the great gate of Whitehall. Others were lighted before the doors of Roman Catholic peers. Lord Arundell of Wardour wisely quieted the mob with a little money; but at Salisbury House in the Strand, an attempt at resistance was made. Lord Salisbury's servants sallied out and fired: but they killed only the unfortunate beadle of the parish, who had come thither to put out the fire; and they were soon routed and driven back into the house. None of the spectacles of that night interested the common people so much as one with which they had, a few years before, been familiar, and which they now, after a long interval, enjoyed once more, the burning of the Pope. This once familiar pageant is known to our generation only by descriptions and engravings. A figure, by no means resembling those rude representations of Guy Faux which are still paraded on the fifth of November, but made of wax with some skill, and adorned at no small expense with robes and a tiara, was mounted on a chair resembling that in which the Bishops of Rome are still, on some great festivals, borne through St. Peter's Church to the high altar. His Holiness was generally accompanied by a train of Cardinals and Jesuits. At his ear stood a buffoon disguised as a devil with horns and tail. No rich and zealous Protestant grudged his guinea on such an occasion, and, if rumour could be trusted, the cost of the procession was sometimes not less than a thousand pounds. After the Pope had been borne some time in state over the heads of the multitude, he was committed to the flames with loud acclamations. In the time of the popularity of Oates and Shaftesbury, this show was exhibited annually in Fleet Street before the windows of the Whig Club on the anniversary of the birth of Queen Elizabeth. Such was the celebrity of these grotesque rites, that Barillon once risked his life in order to peep at them from a hiding place. But from the day when the Rye House plot was discovered, till the day of the acquittal of the Bishops, the ceremony had been disused. Now, however, several Popes made their appearance in different parts of London. The Nuncio was much shocked; and the King was more hurt by this insult to his Church than by all the other affronts which he had received. The magistrates, however, could do nothing. The Sunday had dawned, and the bells of the parish churches were ringing for early prayers, before the fires began to languish and the crowd to disperse. A proclamation was speedily put forth against the rioters. Many of them, mostly young apprentices, were apprehended; but the bills were thrown out at the Middlesex sessions. The Justices, many of whom were Roman Catholics, expostulated with the grand jury and sent them three or four times back, but to no purpose.

Meanwhile the glad tidings were flying to every part of the kingdom, and were everywhere received with raptures. Gloucester, Bedford, and Lichfield were among the places which were distinguished with peculiar zeal: but Bristol and Norwich, which stood nearest to London in population and wealth, approached nearest to London in enthusiasm on this joyful occasion.

The prosecution of the Bishops is an event which stands by itself in our history. It was the first and the last occasion on which two feelings of tremendous potency, two feelings which have generally been opposed to each other, and either of which, when strongly excited, had sufficed to convulse the state, were united in perfect harmony. Those feelings were the love of the Church and love of freedom. During many generations every violent outbreak of High Church feeling, with one exception, has been unfavourable to civil liberty; every violent outbreak of zeal for liberty, with one exception, has been unfavourable to the authority and influence of the prelacy and the priesthood. In 1688 the cause of the hierarchy was for a moment that of the popular party. More than nine thousand clergymen, with the Primate and his most respectable suffragans at their head, offered themselves to endure bonds and the spoiling of their goods for the great fundamental principle of our free constitution. The effect was a coalition which included the most zealous Cavaliers, the most zealous Republicans, and all the intermediate sections of the community. The spirit which had supported Hampden in the preceding generation, the spirit which, in the succeeding generation, supported Sacheverell, combined to support the Archbishop who was Hampden and Sacheverell in one. Those classes of society which are most deeply interested in the preservation of order, which in troubled times are generally most ready to strengthen the hands of government, and which have a natural antipathy to agitators, followed, without scruple, the guidance of a venerable man, the first peer of the Parliament, the first minister of the Church, a Tory in politics, a saint in manners, whom tyranny had in his own despite turned into a demagogue. Many, on the other hand, who had always abhorred episcopacy, as a relic of Popery, and as an instrument of arbitrary power, now asked on bended knees the blessing of a prelate who was ready to wear fetters and to lay his aged limbs on bare stones rather than betray the interests of the Protestant religion and set the prerogative above the laws. With love of the Church and with love of freedom was mingled, at this great crisis, a third feeling which is among the most honourable peculiarities of our national character An individual oppressed by power, even when destitute of all claim to public respect and gratitude, generally finds strong sympathy among us. Thus, in the time of our grandfathers, society was thrown into confusion by the persecution of Wilkes. We have ourselves seen the nation roused to madness by the wrongs of Queen Caroline. It is probably, therefore, that, even if no great political or religious interest had been staked on the event of the proceeding against the Bishops, England would not have seen, without strong emotions of pity and anger, old men of stainless virtue pursued by the vengeance of a harsh and inexorable prince who owed to their fidelity the crown which he wore.

Actuated by these sentiments our ancestors arrayed themselves against the government in one huge and compact mass. All ranks, all parties, all Protestant sects, made up this vast phalanx. In the van were the Lords Spiritual and Temporal. Then came the landed gentry and the clergy, both the Universities, all the Inns of Court, merchants, shopkeepers, farmers, the porters who plied in the streets of the great towns, the peasants who ploughed the fields. The league against the King included the very foremost men who manned his ships, the very sentinels who guarded his palace. The names of Whig and Tory were for a moment forgotten. The old Exclusionist took the old Abhorrer by the hand. Episcopalians, Presbyterians, Independents, Baptists, forgot their long feud, and remembered only their common Protestantism and their common danger. Divines bred in the school of Laud talked loudly, not only of toleration, but of comprehension. The Archbishop soon after his acquittal put forth a pastoral letter which is one of the most remarkable compositions of that age. He had, from his youth up, been at war with the Nonconformists, and had repeatedly assailed them with unjust and unchristian asperity. His principal work was a hideous caricature of the Calvinistic theology. He had drawn up for the thirtieth of January and for the twenty-ninth of May[6] forms of prayer which reflected on the Puritans in language so strong that the government had thought fit to soften it down. But now his heart melted and opened. He solemnly enjoined the Bishops and clergy to have a very tender regard to their brethren the Protestant Dissenters, to visit them often, to entertain them hospitably, to discourse with them civilly, to persuade them, if it might be, to confirm to the Church, but, if that were found impossible, to join them heartily and affectionately in exertions for the blessed cause of the Reformation.

Many pious persons in subsequent years remembered that time with bitter regret. They described it as a short glimpse of a golden age between two iron ages. Such lamentation, though natural, was not reasonable. The coalition of 1688 was produced, and could be produced, only by tyranny which approached to insanity, and by danger which threatened at once all the great institutions of the country. If there has never since been similar union, the reason is that there has never since been similar misgovernment. It must be remembered that, though concord is in itself better than discord, discord may indicate a better state of things than is indicated by concord. Calamity and peril often force men to combine. Prosperity and security often encourage them to separate.

The acquittal of the Bishops was not the only event which makes the thirtieth of June 1688 a great epoch in history. On that day, while the bells of a hundred churches were ringing, while multitudes were busied, from Hyde Park to Mile End, in piling faggots and dressing Popes for the rejoicings of the night, was despatched from London to the Hague an instrument scarcely less important to the liberties of England than the Great Charter.

The prosecution of the Bishops, and the birth of the Prince of Wales, had produced a great revolution in the feelings of many Tories. At the very moment at which their Church was suffering the last excess of injury and insult, they were compelled to renounce the hope of peaceful deliverance. Hitherto they had flattered themselves that the trial to which their loyalty was subjected would, though severe, be temporary, and that their wrongs would shortly be redressed without any violation of the ordinary rule of succession. A very different prospect was now before them. As far as they could look forward they saw only misgovernment, such as that of the last three years, extending through ages. The cradle of their heir apparent to the crown was surrounded by Jesuits. Deadly hatred of that Church of which he would one day be the head would be studiously instilled into his infant mind, would be the guiding principle of his life, and would be bequeathed by him to his posterity. This vista of calamities had no end. It stretched beyond the life of the youngest man living, beyond the eighteenth century. None could say how many generations of Protestant Englishmen might have to bear oppression, such as, even when it had been believed to be short, had been found almost insupportable. Was there then no remedy? One remedy there was, quick, sharp, and decisive, a remedy which the Whigs had been but too ready to employ, but which had always been regarded by the Tories as, in all cases, unlawful.

The Whigs saw that their time was come. Whether they should draw the sword against the government had, during six or seven years, been, in their view, merely a question of prudence; and prudence itself now urged them to take a bold course.

In May, before the birth of the Prince of Wales, and while it was still uncertain whether the Declaration would or would not be read in the churches, Edward Russell had repaired to the Hague. He had strongly represented to the Prince of Orange the state of the public mind, and had advised His Highness to appear in England at the head of a strong body of troops, and to call the people to arms.

William had seen, at a glance, the whole importance of the crisis. "Now or never," he exclaimed in Latin to Van Dykvelt. To Russell he held more guarded language, admitted that the distempers of the state were such as required an extraordinary remedy, but spoke with earnestness of the chance of failure, and of the calamities which failure might bring on Britain and on Europe. He knew well that many who talked in high language about sacrificing their lives and fortunes for their country would hesitate when the prospect of another Bloody Circuit was brought close to them. He wanted therefore to have, not vague professions of good will, but distinct invitations and promises of support subscribed by powerful and eminent men. Russell remarked that it would be dangerous to entrust the design to a great number of persons. William assented, and said that a few signatures would be sufficient, if they were the signatures of statesmen who represented great interests.

With this answer Russell returned to London, where he found the excitement greatly increased and daily increasing. The imprisonment of the Bishops and the delivery of the Queen made his task easier than he could have anticipated. He lost no time in collecting the voices of the chiefs of the opposition.

During June the meetings of those who were in the secret were frequent. At length, on the last day of the month, the day on which the Bishops were pronounced not guilty, the decisive step was taken. A formal invitation, transcribed by Sidney, but drawn up by some person better skilled than Sidney in the art of composition, was despatched to the Hague. In this paper William was assured that nineteen twentieths of the English people were desirous of a change, and would willingly join to effect it, if only they could obtain the help of such a force from abroad as might secure those who should rise in arms from the danger of being dispersed and slaughtered before they could form themselves into anything like military order. If His Highness would appear in the island at the head of some troops, tens of thousands would hasten to his standard. He would soon find himself at the head of a force greatly superior to the whole regular army of England. Nor could that army be implicitly depended on by the government. The officers were discontented; and the common soldiers shared that aversion to Popery which was general in the class from which they were taken. In the navy Protestant feeling was still stronger. It was important to take some decisive step while things were in this state. The enterprise would be far more arduous if it were deferred till the King, by remodelling boroughs and regiments, had procured a Parliament and an army on which he could rely. The conspirators, therefore, implored the Prince to come among them with as little delay as possible. They pledged their honour that they would join him; and they undertook to secure the cooperation of as large a number of persons as could safely be trusted with so momentous and perilous a secret. On one point they thought it their duty to remonstrate with His Highness. He had not taken advantage of the opinion which the great body of the English people had formed touching the late birth. He had, on the contrary, sent congratulations to Whitehall, and had thus seemed to acknowledge that the child who was called Prince of Wales was rightful heir of the throne. This was a grave error, and had damped the zeal of many. Not one person in a thousand doubted that the boy was supposititious; and the Prince would be wanting to his own interests if the suspicious circumstances which had attended the Queen's confinement were not put prominently forward among his reasons for taking arms.

This paper was signed in cipher by the seven chiefs of the conspiracy, Shrewsbury, Devonshire, Danby, Lumley, Compton, Russell, and Sidney. Herbert undertook to be their messenger. His errand was one of no ordinary peril. He assumed the garb of a common sailor, and in this disguise reached the Dutch coast in safety, on the Friday after the trial of the Bishops. He instantly hastened to the Prince. Bentinck and Van Dykvelt were summoned, and several days were passed in deliberation.

And now the Hague was crowded with British adventurers of all the various factions which the tyranny of James had united in a strange coalition, old royalists who had shed their blood for the throne, old agitators of the army of the

Parliament, Tories who had been persecuted in the days of the Exclusion Bill, Whigs who had fled to the Continent for their share in the Rye House plot.

The difference between the expedition of 1685 and the expedition of 1688 was sufficiently marked by the difference between the manifestoes which the leaders of those expeditions published. For Monmouth Ferguson[7] had scribbled an absurd and brutal libel about the burning of London, the strangling of Godfrey, the butchering of Essex, and the poisoning of Charles. The Declaration of William was drawn up by the Grand Pensionary Fagel, who was highly renowned as a publicist. Though weighty and learned, it was, in its original form, much too prolix: but it was abridged and translated into English by Burnet, who well understood the art of popular composition. It began by a solemn preamble, setting forth that, in every community, the strict observance of law was necessary alike to the happiness of nations and to the security of governments. The Prince of Orange had therefore seen with deep concern that the fundamental laws of a kingdom, with which he was by blood and by marriage closely connected, had, by the advice of evil counsellors, been grossly and systematically violated. The power of dispensing with Acts of Parliament had been strained to such a point that the whole legislative authority had been transferred to the crown. Decisions at variance with the spirit of the constitution had been obtained from the tribunals by turning out Judge after Judge, till the bench had been filled with men ready to obey implicitly the directions of the government. Notwithstanding the King's repeated assurances that he would maintain the established religion, persons notoriously hostile to that religion had been promoted, not only to civil offices, but also to ecclesiastical benefices. The government of the Church had, in defiance of express statues, been entrusted to a new court of High Commission; and in that court an avowed Papist had a seat. Good subjects, for refusing to violate their duty and their oaths, had been ejected from their property, in contempt of the Great Charter of the liberties of England. Meanwhile persons who could not legally set foot on the island had been placed at the head of seminaries for the corruption of youth. Lieutenants, Deputy Lieutenants, Justices of the Peace, had been dismissed in multitudes for refusing to support a pernicious and unconstitutional policy. The franchises of almost every borough in the realm had been invaded. The courts of justice were in such a state that their decisions, even in civil matters, had ceased to inspire confidence, and that their servility in criminal cases had brought on the kingdom the stain of innocent blood. All these abuses, loathed by the English nation, were to be defended, it seemed, by an army of Irish Papists. Nor was this all. The most arbitrary princes had never accounted it an offence in a subject modestly and peaceably to represent his grievances and to ask for relief. But supplication was now treated as a high misdemeanour in England. For no crime but that of offering to a Sovereign a petition drawn up in the most respectful terms, the father of the Church had been imprisoned and prosecuted; and every Judge who had given his voice in their favour had instantly been turned out. The calling of a free and lawful Parliament might indeed be an effectual remedy for all these evils; but such a Parliament, unless the whole spirit of the administration was changed, the nation could not hope to see. It was evidently the intention of the Court to bring together, by means of a regulated corporation and of Popish returning officers, a body which would be a House of Commons in name alone. Lastly, there were circumstances which raised a grave suspicion that the child who was called Prince of Wales was not really born of the Queen. For these reasons the Prince, mindful of his near relation to the royal house, and grateful for the affection which the English people had ever shown to his beloved wife and to himself, had resolved in compliance with the request of many Lords Spiritual and Temporal, and of many other persons of all ranks, to go over at the head of a force sufficient to repel violence. He abjured all thought of conquest. He protested that, while his troops remained in the island, they should be kept under the strictest restraints of discipline, and that, as soon as the nation had been delivered from tyranny, they should be sent back. His single object was to have a free and legal Parliament assembled: and to the decision of such a Parliament he solemnly pledged himself to leave all questions both public and private.

As soon as copies of this Declaration were handed about the Hague, signs of dissension began to appear among the English. Wildman, indefatigable in mischief, prevailed on some of his countrymen, and, among others, on the headstrong and volatile Mordaunt, to declare that they would not take up arms on such grounds. The paper had been drawn up merely to please the Cavaliers and the parsons. The injuries of the Church and the trial of the Bishops had been put too prominently forward; and nothing had been said of the tyrannical manner in which the Tories, before their rupture with the Court, had treated the Whigs. Wildman then brought forward a counterproject, prepared by himself, which, if it had been adopted, would have disgusted all the

Anglican clergy and four fifths of the landed aristocracy. The leading Whigs strongly opposed him. Russell in particular declared that, if such an insane course were taken, there would be an end of the coalition from which alone the nation could expect deliverance. The dispute was at length settled by the authority of William, who, with his usual good sense determined that the manifesto should stand nearly as Fagel and Burnet had framed it.

On the sixteenth of October, according to the English reckoning, was held a solemn sitting of the States of Holland. The Prince came to bid them farewell. He thanked them for the kindness with which they had watched over him when he was left an orphan child, for the confidence which they had reposed in him during his administration, and for the assistance which they had granted him at this momentous crisis. He entreated them to believe that he had always meant and endeavoured to promote the interest of his country. He was now quitting them, perhaps never to return. If he should fall in defence of the reformed religion and of the independence of Europe, he commended his beloved wife to their care. The Grand Pensionary answered in a faltering voice; and in all that grave senate there was none who could refrain from shedding tears. But the iron stoicism of William never gave way; and he stood among his weeping friends calm and austere as if he had been about to leave them only for a short visit to his hunting grounds at Loo.

The deputies of the principal towns accompanied him to his yacht. Even the representatives of Amsterdam, so long the chief seat of opposition to his administration, joined in paying him this compliment. Public prayers were offered for him on that day in all the churches of the Hague.

In the evening he arrived at Helvoetsluys and went on board of a frigate called the Brill. His flag was immediately hoisted. It displayed the arms of Nassau quartered with those of England. The motto, embroidered in letters three feet long, was happily chosen. The House of Orange had long used the elliptical device, "I will maintain." The ellipsis was now filled up with words of high import, "The liberties of England and the Protestant religion."

The Prince had not been many hours on board when the wind became fair. On the nineteenth the armament put out to sea, and traversed, before a strong breeze, about half the distance between the Dutch and English coasts. Then the wind changed, blew hard from the west, and swelled into a violent tempest. The ships, scattered and in great distress, regained the shore of Holland as they best might. The Brill reached Helvoetsluys on the twenty-first. The Prince's fellow passengers had observed with admiration that neither peril nor mortification had for one moment disturbed his composure. He now, though suffering from sea sickness, refused to go on shore: for he conceived that, by remaining on board, he should in the most effectual manner notify to Europe that the late misfortune had only delayed for a very short time the execution of his purpose. In two or three days the fleet reassembled. One vessel only had been cast away. Not a single soldier or sailor was missing. Some horses had perished: but this loss the Prince with great expedition repaired; and before the London Gazette had spread the news of his mishap, he was again ready to sail.

His Declaration preceded him only by a few hours. On the first of November it began to be mentioned in mysterious whispers by the politicians of London, was passed secretly from man to man, and was slipped into the boxes of the post office. One of the agents was arrested, and the packets of which he was in charge were carried to Whitehall. The King read, and was greatly troubled. His first impulse was to hide the paper from all human eyes. He threw into the fire every copy which had been brought to him, except one; and that one he would scarcely trust out of his own hands.

The paragraph in the manifesto which disturbed him the most was that in which it was said that some of the Peers, Spiritual and Temporal, had invited the Prince of Orange to invade England. Halifax, Clarendon, and Nottingham were then in London. They were immediately summoned to the palace and interrogated. Halifax, though conscious of innocence, refused at first to make any answer. "Your Majesty asks me," said he, "whether I have committed high treason. If I am suspected, let me be brought before my peers. And how can your Majesty place any dependence on the answer of a culprit whose life is at stake? Even if I had invited His Highness over, I should without scruple plead Not Guilty." The King declared that he did not at all consider Halifax as a culprit, and that he had asked the question as one gentleman asks another who has been calumniated whether there be the least foundation for the calumny. "In that case," said Halifax, "I have no objection to aver, as a gentleman speaking to a gentleman, on my honour, which is sacred as my oath, that I have not invited the Prince of Orange over." Clarendon and Nottingham said the same. The King was still more anxious to ascertain the temper of the Prelates. If they were hostile to him, his throne was indeed in danger. But it could not be. There was something monstrous in the supposition that any Bishop of the Church of England could rebel against his

Sovereign. Compton was called into the royal closet, and was asked whether he believed that there was the slightest ground for the Prince's assertion. The Bishop was in a strait; for he himself was one of the seven who had signed the invitation; and his conscience, not a very enlightened conscience, would not suffer him, it seems, to utter a direct falsehood. "Sir," he said, "I am quite confident that there is not one of my brethren who is not as guiltless as myself in this matter." The equivocation was ingenious: but whether the difference between the sin of such an equivocation and the sin of a lie be worth any expense of ingenuity may perhaps be doubted. The King was satisfied. "I fully acquit you all," he said. "But I think it necessary that you should publicly contradict the slanderous charge brought against you in the Prince's Declaration." The Bishop very naturally begged that he might be allowed to read the paper which he was required to contradict: but the King would not suffer him to look at it.

On the following day appeared a proclamation threatening with the severest punishment all who should circulate, or who should even dare to read William's manifesto. The Primate and the few Spiritual Peers who happened to be then in London had orders to wait upon the King. Preston was in attendance with the Prince's Declaration in his hand. "My Lords," said James, "listen to this passage. It concerns you." Preston then read the sentence in which the Spiritual Peers were mentioned. The King proceeded: "I do not believe one word of this: I am satisfied of your innocence: but I think it fit to let you know of what you are accused."

The Primate, with many dutiful expressions, protested that the King did him no more than justice. "I was born in

Your Majesty's allegiance. I have repeatedly confirmed that allegiance by my oath. I can have but one King at a time. I have not invited the Prince over; and I do not believe that a single one of my brethren has done so." "I am sure I have not," said Crewe of Durham. "Nor I," said Cartwright of Chester. Crewe and Cartwright might well be believed; for both had sate in the Ecclesiastical Commission. When Compton's turn came, he parried the question with an adroitness which a Jesuit might have envied. "I gave Your Majesty my answer yesterday."

James repeated again and again that he fully acquitted them all. Nevertheless it would, in his judgement, be for his service and for their own honour that they should publicly vindicate themselves. He therefore required them to draw up a paper setting forth their abhorrence of the Prince's design. They remained silent: their silence was supposed to imply consent; and they were suffered to withdraw.

Meanwhile the fleet of William was on the German Ocean. It was on the evening of Thursday the first of November that he put to sea the second time. The wind blew fresh from the east. The armament, during twelve hours, held a course towards the northwest. The light vessels sent out by the English Admiral for the purpose of obtaining intelligence brought back news which confirmed the prevailing opinion that the enemy would try to land in Yorkshire. All at once, on a signal from the Prince's ship, the whole fleet tacked, and made sail for the British Channel. The same breeze which favoured the voyage of the invaders, prevented Dartmouth from coming out of the Thames. His ships were forced to strike yards and topmasts; and two of his frigates, which had gained the open sea, were shattered by the violence of the weather and driven back into the river.

The Dutch fleet ran fast before the gale, and reached the Straits at about ten in the morning of Saturday, the third of November. William himself, in the Brill, led the way. More than six hundred vessels, with canvas spread to a favourable wind, followed in his train. The transports were in the centre. The men of war, more than fifty in number, formed an outer rampart. Herbert, with the title of Lieutenant Admiral General, commanded the whole fleet. His post was in the rear, and many English sailors, inflamed against Popery, and attracted by high pay, served under him. It was not without difficulty that the Prince had prevailed on some Dutch officers of high reputation to submit to the authority of a stranger. But the arrangement was eminently judicious. There was, in the King's fleet, much discontent and an ardent zeal for the Protestant faith. But within the memory of old mariners the Dutch and English navies had thrice, with heroic spirit and various fortune, contended for the empire of the sea. Our sailors had not forgotten the broom with which Tromp had threatened to sweep the Channel, or the fire which De Ruyter had lighted in the dockyards of the Medway. Had the rival nations been once more brought face to face on the element of which both claimed the sovereignty, all other thoughts might have given place to mutual animosity. A bloody and obstinate battle might have been fought. Defeat would have been fatal to William's enterprise. Even victory would have deranged all his deeply meditated schemes of policy. He therefore wisely determined that the pursuers, if they overtook him, should be hailed in their own mother tongue, and adjured, by an admiral under whom they had served, and whom they esteemed, not to fight against old messmates for Popish tyranny. Such an appeal might possibly avert a conflict. If a conflict took place, one English commander would be opposed to another; nor would the pride of the islanders be wounded by learning that Dartmouth had been compelled to strike to Herbert.

Happily William's precautions were not necessary. Soon after midday he passed the Straits. His fleet spread to within a league of Dover on the north and of Calais on the south. The men of war on the extreme right and left saluted both fortresses at once. The troops appeared under arms on the decks. The flourish of trumpets, the clash of cymbals, and the rolling of drums were distinctly heard at once on the English and French shores. An innumerable company of gazers blackened the white beach of Kent. Another mighty multitude covered the coast of Picardy. Rapin de Thoyras, who, driven by persecution from his country, had taken service in the Dutch army, and now went with the Prince to England, described the spectacle, many years later, as the most magnificent and affecting that was ever seen by human eyes. At sunset the armament was off Beachy Head. Then the lights were kindled. The sea was in a blaze for many miles. But the eyes of all the steersmen were directed throughout the night to three huge lanterns which flamed on the stern of the Brill.

Meanwhile a courier had been riding post from Dover Castle to Whitehall with news that the Dutch had passed the Straits and were steering westward. It was necessary to make an immediate change in all the military arrangements. Messengers were despatched in every direction. Officers were roused from their beds at dead of night. At three on the

Sunday morning there was a great muster by torchlight in Hyde Park. The King had sent several regiments northward in the expectation that William would land in Yorkshire. Expresses were despatched to recall them. All the forces except those which were necessary to keep the peace of the capital were ordered to move to the West. Salisbury was appointed as the place of rendezvous; but, as it was thought possible that Portsmouth might be the first point of attack, three battalions of guards and a strong body of cavalry set out for that fortress. In a few hours it was known that Portsmouth was safe; and these troops then received orders to change their route and to hasten to Salisbury.

When Sunday the fourth of November dawned, the cliffs of the Isle of Wight were full in view of the Dutch armament. That day was the anniversary both of William's birth and of his marriage. Sail was slackened during part of the morning; and divine service was performed on board of the ships. In the afternoon and through the night the fleet held on its course. Torbay was the place where the Prince intended to land. But the morning of Monday the fifth of November was hazy. The pilot of the Brill could not discern the sea marks, and carried the fleet too far to the west. The danger was great. To return in the face of the wind was impossible. Plymouth was the next port. But at Plymouth a garrison had been posted under the command of the Earl of Bath. The landing might be opposed: and a check might produce serious consequences. There could be little doubt, moreover that at this time the royal fleet had got out of the Thames and was hastening full sail down the Channel. Russell saw the whole extent of the peril, and exclaimed to Burnet, "You may go to prayers, Doctor. All is over." At that moment the wind changed: a soft breeze sprang up from the south: the mist dispersed: the sun shone forth; and, under the mild light of an autumnal noon, the fleet turned back, passed round the lofty cape of Berry Head, and rode safe in the harbour of Torbay.

Since William looked on that harbour its aspect has greatly changed. The amphitheatre which surrounds the spacious basin, now exhibits everywhere the signs of prosperity and civilisation. At the northeastern extremity has sprung up a great watering place, to which strangers are attracted from the most remote parts of our island by the Italian softness of the air: for in that climate the myrtle flourishes unsheltered, and even the winter is milder than the Northumbrian April. The inhabitants are about ten thousand in number. The newly built churches and chapels, the baths and libraries, the hotels and public gardens, the infirmary and the museum, the white streets, rising terrace above terrace, the gay villas peeping from the midst of shrubberies and flower beds, present a spectacle widely different from any that in the seventeenth century England could show. At the opposite end of the bay lies, sheltered by Berry Head, the stirring market town of Brixham, the wealthiest seat of our fishing trade. A pier and a haven were formed there at the beginning of the present century, but have been found insufficient for the increasing traffic. The population is about six thousand souls. The shipping amounts to more than two hundred sail. The tonnage exceeds many times the tonnage of the port of Liverpool under the kings of the House of Stuart. But Torbay, when the Dutch fleet cast anchor there, was known only as a haven where ships sometimes took refuge from the tempests of the Atlantic. Its quiet shores were undisturbed by the bustle either of commerce or of pleasure; and the huts of ploughmen and fishermen were thinly scattered over what is now the site of crowded marts and of luxurious pavilions.

The peasantry of the coast of Devonshire remembered the name of Monmouth with affection, and held Popery in detestation. They therefore crowded down to the seaside with provisions and offers of service. The disembarkation instantly commenced. Sixty boats conveyed the troops to the coast. Mackay was sent on shore first with the British regiments. The Prince soon followed. He landed where the quay of Brixham now stands. The whole aspect of the place has been altered. Where we now see a port crowded with shipping, and a market place swarming with buyers and sellers, the waves then broke on a desolate beach; but a fragment of the rock on which the deliverer stepped from his boat has been carefully preserved, and is set up as an object of public veneration in the centre of that busy wharf.

As soon as the Prince had planted his foot on dry ground he called for horses. Two beasts, such as the small yeoman of that time were in the habit of riding, were procured from the neighbouring village. William and Schomberg mounted and proceeded to examine the country.

As soon as Burnet[8] was on shore he hastened to the Prince. An amusing dialogue took place between them. Burnet poured forth his congratulations with genuine delight, and then eagerly asked what were His Highness's plans. Military men are seldom disposed to take counsel with gownsmen on military matters; and William regarded the interference of unprofessional advisors, in questions relating to war with even more than the disgust ordinarily felt by soldiers on such occasions. But he was at that moment in an excellent humour, and, instead of signifying his displeasure by a short and cutting reprimand, graciously extended his hand, and answered his chaplain's question by another question: "Well Doctor, what do you think of predestination now?" The reproof was so delicate that Burnet, whose perceptions were not very fine, did not perceive it. He answered with great fervour that he should never forget the signal manner in which Providence had favoured their undertaking.

During the first day the troops who had gone on shore had many discomforts to endure. The earth was soaked with rain. The baggage was still on board of the ships. Officers of high rank were compelled to sleep in wet clothes on the wet ground: the Prince himself had not better quarters than a hut afforded. His banner was displayed on the thatched roof; and some bedding brought from the Brill was spread for him on the floor. There was some difficulty about handling the horses; and it seemed probably that this operation would occupy several days. But on the following morning the prospect cleared. The wind was gentle. The water in the bay was as even as glass. Some fishermen pointed out a place where the ships could be brought within sixty feet of the beach. This was done; and in three hours many hundreds of horses swam safely to shore.

The disembarkation had hardly been effected when the wind rose again, and swelled into a fierce gale from the west. The enemy coming in pursuit down the Channel had been stopped by the same change of weather which enabled William to land. During two days the King's fleet lay on an unruffled sea in sight of Beachy Head. At length Dartmouth was able to proceed. He passed the Isle of Wight, and one of his ships came in sight of the Dutch topmasts in Torbay. Just at this moment he was encountered by the tempest, and compelled to take shelter in the harbour of Portsmouth. At that time James, who was not incompetent to form a judgement on a question of seamanship, declared himself perfectly satisfied that his admiral had done all that man could do, and had yielded only to the irresistible hostility of the winds and waves. At a later period the unfortunate prince began, with little reason, to suspect Dartmouth of treachery, or at least of slackness.

The weather had indeed served the Protestant cause so well that some men of more piety than judgement fully believed the ordinary laws of nature to have been suspended for the preservation of the liberty and religion of England. Exactly a hundred years before, they said, the Armada, invincible by man, had been scattered by the wrath of God. Civil freedom and divine truth were again in jeopardy, and again the obedient elements had fought for the good cause. The wind had blown strong from the east while the Prince wished to sail down the Channel, had turned to the south when he wished to enter Torbay, had sunk to a calm during the disembarkation, and as soon as the disembarkation was completed, had risen to a storm, and had met the pursuers in the face. Nor did men omit to remark that, by an extraordinary coincidence, the Prince had reached our shores on a day on which the Church of England commemorated, by prayer and thanksgiving, the wonderful escape of the Royal House and of the three estates from the blackest plot ever devised by Papists. Carstairs, whose suggestions were sure to meet with attention from the Prince, recommended that, as soon as the landing had been effected, public thanks should be offered to God for the protection so conspicuously accorded to the great enterprise. This advice was taken, and with excellent effect. The troops, taught to regard themselves as favourites of heaven, were inspired with new courage; and the English people formed the most favourable opinion of a general and an army so attentive to the duties of religion.

On Tuesday, the sixth of November, William's army began to march up the country. Some regiments advanced as far as Newton Abbot. A stone, set up in the midst of that little town, still marks the spot where the Prince's Declaration was solemnly read to the people. The movements of the troops were slow: for the rain fell in torrents, and the roads of England were then in a state which seemed frightful to persons accustomed to the excellent communications of Holland. William took up his quarters, during two days, at Ford, a seat of the ancient and illustrious family of Courtenay, in the neighbourhood of Newton Abbot. He was magnificently lodged and feasted there: but it is remarkable that the owner of the house, though a strong Whig, did not choose to be the first to put life and fortune in peril, and cautiously abstained from doing anything which, if the King should prevail, could be treated as a crime.

Exeter, in the meantime, was greatly agitated. Lamplugh, the bishop, as soon as he heard that the Dutch were at Torbay, set off in terror for London. The Dean fled from the deanery. The magistrates were for the King, the body of the inhabitants for the Prince. Everything was in confusion when, on the morning of Thursday, the eighth of November, a body of troops, under the command of Mordaunt, appeared before the city. With Mordaunt came Burnet, to whom William had entrusted the duty of protecting the clergy of the Cathedral from injury and insult. The Mayor and Aldermen had ordered the gates to be closed, but yielded on the first summons. The deanery was prepared for the reception of the Prince. On the following day, Friday the ninth, he arrived. The magistrates had been pressed to receive him in state at the entrance of the city, but had steadfastly refused. The pomp of that day, however, could well spare them. Such a sight had never been seen in Devonshire. Many of the citizens went forth half a day's journey to meet the champion of their religion. All the neighbouring villages poured forth their inhabitants. A great crowd, consisting chiefly of young peasants, brandishing their cudgels, had assembled on the top of Haldon Hill, whence the army, marching from Chudleigh, first descried the rich valley of the Exe, and the two massive towers rising from the cloud of smoke which overhung the capital of the West. The road, all down the long descent, and through the plain to the banks of the river, was lined, mile after mile, with spectators. From the West Gate to the Cathedral Close, the pressing and shouting on each side was such as reminded Londoners of the crowds on the Lord Mayor's day. The houses were gaily decorated. Doors, windows, balconies, and roofs were thronged with gazers. An eye accustomed to the pomp of war would have found much to criticise in the spectacle. For several toilsome marches in the rain, through roads where one who travelled on foot sank at every step up to the ankles in clay, had not improved the appearance either of the men or of their accoutrements. But the people of Devonshire, altogether unused to the splendour of well ordered camps, were overwhelmed with delight and awe. Descriptions of the martial pageant were circulated all over the kingdom. They contained much that was well fitted to gratify the vulgar appetite for the marvellous. For the Dutch army, composed of men who had been born in various climates, and had served under various standards, presented an aspect at once grotesque, gorgeous, and terrible to islanders who had, in general, a very indistinct notion of foreign countries. First rode Macclesfield at the head of two hundred gentlemen, mostly of English blood, glittering in helmets and cuirasses, and mounted on Flemish war horses. Each was attended by a negro, brought from the sugar plantations on the coast of Guiana. The citizens of Exeter, who had never seen so many specimens of the African race, gazed with wonder on those black faces set off by embroidered turbans and white feathers. Then, with drawn broadswords, came a squadron of Swedish horsemen in black armour and fur cloaks. They were regarded with a strange interest; for it was rumoured that they were natives of a land where the ocean was frozen and where the night lasted through half the year, and that they had themselves slain the huge bears whose skins they wore. Next, surrounded by a goodly company of gentlemen and pages, was borne aloft the Prince's banner. On its broad folds the crowd which covered the roofs and filled the windows read with delight that memorable inscription, "The Protestant religion and the liberties of England." But the acclamations redoubled when, attended by forty running footmen, the Prince himself appeared, armed on back and breast, wearing a white plume and mounted on a white charger. With how martial an air he curbed his horse, how thoughtful and commanding was the expression of his ample forehead and falcon eye, may still be seen on the canvas of Kneller. Once those grave features relaxed into a smile. It was when an ancient woman, perhaps one of the zealous Puritans who, through twenty-eight years of persecution, had waited with firm faith for the consolation of Israel, perhaps the mother of some rebel who had perished in the carnage of Sedgemoor, or in the more fearful carnage of the Bloody Circuit, broke from the crowd, rushed through the drawn swords and curvetting horses, touched the hand of the deliverer, and cried out that now she was happy. Near to the Prince was one who divided with him the gaze of the multitude. That, men said, was the great Count Schomberg, the first soldier in Europe, since Turenne and Condé were gone, the man whose genius and valour had saved the Portuguese monarchy on the field of Montes Claros, the man who had earned a still higher glory by resigning the truncheon of a Marshal of France for the sake of the true religion. It was not forgotten that the two heroes who, indissolubly united by their common Protestantism, were entering Exeter together, had twelve years before been opposed to each other under the walls of Maestricht, and that the energy of the young Prince had not then been found a match for the cool science of the veteran who now rode in friendship by his side. Then came a long column of the whiskered infantry of Switzerland, distinguished in all the Continental wars of two centuries by preeminent valour and discipline, but never till that week seen on English ground. And then marched a succession of bands, designated, as was the fashion of that age, after their leaders, Bentinck, Solmes, and Ginkell, Talmash and Mackay. With peculiar pleasure Englishmen might look on one gallant regiment which still bore the name of the honoured and lamented Ossory. The effect of the spectacle was heightened by the recollection of more than one renowned event in which the warriors now pouring through the West Gate had borne a share. For they had seen service very different from that of the Devonshire militia, or of the camp at Hounslow. Some of them had repelled the fiery onset of the French on the field of Seneff; and others had crossed swords with the infidels in the cause of Christendom on that great day when the siege of Vienna was raised. The very senses of the multitude were fooled by imagination. Newsletters conveyed to every part of the kingdom fabulous accounts of the size and strength of the invaders. It was affirmed that they were, with scarcely an exception, above six feet high, and that they wielded such huge pikes, swords, and muskets, as had never before been seen in England. Nor did the wonder of the population diminish when the artillery arrived, twenty-one heavy pieces of brass cannon, which were with difficulty tugged along by sixteen cart horses to each. Much curiosity was excited by a strange structure mounted on wheels. It proved to be a movable smithy, furnished with all tools and materials necessary for repairing arms and carriages. But nothing caused so much astonishment as the bridge of boats, which was laid with great speed on the Exe for the conveyance of wagons, and afterwards as speedily taken to pieces and carried away. It was made, if report said true, after a pattern contrived by the Christians who were warring against the Great Turk on the Danube. The foreigners inspired as much good will as admiration. Their politic leader took care to distribute the quarters in such a manner as to cause the smallest possible inconvenience to the inhabitants of Exeter and of the neighbouring villages. The most rigid discipline was maintained. Not only were pillage and outrage effectually prevented, but the troops were required to demean themselves with civility towards all classes. Those who had formed their notions of an army from the conduct of Kirke and his Lambs[9] were amazed to see soldiers who never swore at a landlady or took an egg without paying for it. In return for this moderation the people furnished the troops with provisions in great abundance and at reasonable prices.

Much depended on the course which, at this great crisis, the clergy of the Church of England might take; and the members of the Chapter of Exeter were the first who were called upon to declare their sentiments. Burnet informed the Canons, now left without a head by the flight of the Dean, that they could not be permitted to use the prayer for the Prince of Wales, and that a solemn service must be performed in honour of the safe arrival of the Prince. The Canons did not choose to appear in their stalls, but some of the choristers and prebendaries attended. William repaired in military state to the Cathedral. As he passed under the gorgeous screen, that renowned organ, scarcely surpassed by any of those which are the boast of his native Holland, gave out a peal of triumph. He mounted the Bishop's seat, a stately throne rich with the carving of the fifteenth century. Burnet stood below; and a crowd of warriors and nobles appeared on the right hand and on the left. The singers, robed in white, sang the Te Deum. When the chaunt was over, Burnet read the Prince's Declaration; but, as soon as the first words were uttered, prebendaries and singers crowded in all haste out of the choir. At the close Burnet cried in a loud voice, "God save the Prince of Orange!" and many fervent voices answered, "Amen."

On Sunday, the eleventh of November, Burnet preached before the Prince in the Cathedral, and dilated on the signal mercy vouchsafed by God to the English Church and nation. At the same time a singular event happened in a humbler place of worship. Ferguson resolved to preach at the Presbyterian meeting house. The minister and elders would not consent: but the turbulent and halfwitted knave, fancying that the times of Fleetwood and Harrison were come again, forced the door, went through the congregation sword in hand, mounted the pulpit, and there poured forth a fiery invective against the King. The time for such follies had gone by: and this exhibition excited nothing but derision and disgust.

While these things were passing in Devonshire the ferment was great in London. The Prince's Declaration, in spite of all precautions, was now in every man's hands. On the sixth of November James, still uncertain on what part of the coast the invaders had landed, summoned the Primate and three other Bishops, Compton of London, White of Peterborough and Sprat of Rochester, to a conference in the closet. The King listened graciously while the prelates made warm professions of loyalty, and assured them that he did not suspect them. "But where," said he, "is the paper that you were to bring me?" "Sir," answered Sancroft, "we have brought no paper. We are not solicitous to clear our fame to the world. It is no new thing to us to be reviled and falsely accused. Our consciences acquit us: Your Majesty acquits us; and we are satisfied." "Yes," said the King; "but a declaration from you is necessary to my service." He then produced a copy of the Prince's manifesto. "See," he said, "how you are mentioned here." "Sir," answered one of the Bishops, "not one person in five hundred believes this manifesto to be genuine." "No!" cried the King fiercely: "then those five hundred would bring the Prince of Orange to cut my throat." "God forbid," exclaimed the prelates in concert. But the King's understanding, never very clear, was now quite bewildered. One of his peculiarities was that, whenever his opinion was not adopted, he fancied that his veracity was questioned. "This paper not genuine!" he exclaimed, turning over the leaves with his hands. "Am I not worthy to be believed? Is my word not to be taken?" "At all events, sir," said one of the Bishops, "this is not an ecclesiastical matter. It lies within the sphere of the civil power. God has entrusted Your Majesty with the sword: and it is not for us to invade your functions." Then the Archbishop, with that gentle and temperate malice which inflicts the deepest wounds, declared that he must be excused from setting his hand to any political document. "I and my brethren, sir" he said, "have already smarted severely for meddling with affairs of state; and we shall be very cautious how we do so again. We once subscribed a petition of the most harmless kind: we presented it in the most respectful manner; and we found that we had committed a high offence. We were saved from ruin only by the merciful protection of God. And, sir, the ground then taken by Your Majesty's Attorney and Solicitor was that, out of Parliament, we were private men, and that it was criminal presumption in private men to meddle with politics. They attacked us so fiercely that for my part I gave myself over for lost." "I thank you for that, my Lord of Canterbury," said the King: "I should have hoped that you would not have thought yourself lost by falling into my hands." Such a speech might have become the mouth of a merciful sovereign, but it came with a bad grace from a prince who had burned a woman alive for harbouring one of his flying enemies, from a prince round whose knees his own nephew had clung in vain agonies of supplication. The Archbishop was not to be so silenced. He resumed his story, and recounted the insults which the creatures of he Court had offered to the Church of England, among which some ridicule thrown on his own style occupied a conspicuous place. The King had nothing to say but that there was no use in repeating old grievances, and that he had hoped that these things had been quite forgotten. He, who never forgot the smallest injury that he had suffered, could not understand how others should remember for a few weeks the most deadly injuries that he had inflicted.

At length the conversation came back to the point from which it had wandered. The King insisted on having from the Bishops a paper declaring their abhorrence of the Prince's enterprise. They, with many professions of the most submissive loyalty, pertinaciously refused. The Prince, they said, asserted that he had been invited by temporal as well as by spiritual peers. The imputation was common. Why should not the purgation be common also? "I see how it is," said the King. "Some of the temporal peers have been with you, and have persuaded you to cross me in this matter." The Bishops solemnly averred that it was not so. But it would, they said, seem strange that, on a question involving grave political and military considerations, the temporal peers should be entirely passed over, and the prelates alone should be require to take a prominent part. "But this," said James, "is my method. I am your King. It is for me to judge what is best. I will go my own way; and I call on you to assist me."

The Bishops assured him that they would assist him in their proper department, as Christian ministers with their prayers, and as peers of the realm with their advice in his Parliament. James, who wanted neither the prayers of heretics nor the advice of Parliaments, was bitterly disappointed. After a long altercation, "I have done," he said; "I will urge you no further. Since you will not help me, I must trust to myself and to my own arms."

The Bishops had hardly left the royal presence, when a courier arrived with the news that on the preceding day the Prince of Orange had landed in Devonshire. During the following week London was violently agitated. On Sunday, the eleventh of November, a rumour was circulated that knives, gridirons, and caldrons, intended for the torturing of heretics, were concealed in the monastery which had been established under the King's protection at Clerkenwell. Great multitudes assembled round the building, and were about to demolish it, when a military force arrived. The crowd was dispersed, and several of the rioters were slain. An inquest sate on the bodies, and came to a decision which strongly indicated the temper of the public mind. The jury found that certain loyal and well disposed persons, who had gone to put down the meetings of traitors and public enemies at a mass house, had been wilfully murdered by the soldiers; and this strange verdict was signed by all the jurors. The ecclesiastics at Clerkenwell, naturally alarmed by these symptoms of popular feeling, were desirous to place their property in safety. They succeeded in removing most of their furniture before any report of their intentions got abroad. But at length the suspicions of the rabble were excited. The last two carts were stopped in Holborn, and all that they contained was publicly burned in the middle of the street. So great was the alarm among the Catholics that all their places of worship were closed, except those which belonged to the royal family and to foreign Ambassadors.

On the whole, however, things as yet looked not unfavourably for James. The invaders had been more than a week on English ground. Yet no man of note had joined them. No rebellion had broken out in the north or the east. No servant of the crown appeared to have betrayed his trust. The royal army was assembling fast at Salisbury, and, though inferior in discipline to that of William, was superior in numbers.

The Prince was undoubtedly surprised and mortified by the slackness of those who had invited him to England. By the common people of Devonshire, indeed, he had been received with every sign of good will: but no nobleman, no gentleman of high consideration, had yet repaired to his quarters. The explanation of this singular fact is probably to be found in the circumstance that he had landed in a part of the island where he had not been expected. His friends in the north had made their arrangements for a rising, on the supposition that he would be among them with an army. His friends in the west had made no arrangements at all, and were naturally disconcerted at finding themselves suddenly called upon take the lead in a movement so important and perilous. They had also fresh in their recollection, and indeed full in their sight, the disastrous consequences of rebellion, gibbets, heads, mangled quarters, families still in deep mourning for brave sufferers who had loved their country well but not wisely. After a warning so terrible and so recent, some hesitation was natural. It was equally natural, however, that William, who, not trusting to promises from England, had put to hazard, not only his own fame and fortunes, but also the prosperity and independence of his native land, should feel deeply mortified. He was, indeed, so indignant, that he talked of falling back to Torbay, reembarking his troops, returning to Holland, and leaving those who had betrayed him to the fate which they deserved. At length, on Monday, the twelfth of November, a gentleman named Burrington, who resided in the neighbourhood of Crediton, joined the Prince's standard, and his example was followed by several of his neighbours.

While foes were thus rising up all round the King, friends were fast shrinking from his side. The idea of resistance had become familiar to every mind. Many, who had been struck with horror when they heard of the first defections, now blamed themselves for having been so slow to discern the signs of the times. There was no longer any difficulty or danger in repairing to William. The King, in calling on the nation to elect representatives, had, by implication, authorised all men to repair to the places where they had votes or interest; and many of those places were already occupied by invaders or insurgents.

By this time the invaders, steadily though slowly advancing, were within seventy miles of London. Though midwinter was approaching, the weather was fine: the way was pleasant; and the turf of Salisbury Plain seemed luxuriously smooth to men who had been toiling through the miry ruts of the Devonshire and Somersetshire highways. The route of the army lay close to Stonehenge; and regiment after regiment halted to examine that mysterious ruin, celebrated all over the Continent as the greatest wonder of our island. William entered Salisbury with the same military pomp which he had displayed at Exeter, and was lodged there in the palace which the King had occupied a few days before.

Thus far the Prince's enterprise had prospered beyond the anticipations of the most sanguine. And now, according to the general law which governs human affairs, prosperity began to produce disunion. The English assembled at Salisbury were divided into two parties. One party consisted of Whigs who had always regarded the doctrines of passive obedience and of indefeasible hereditary right as slavish superstitions. Many of them had passed years in exile. All had been long shut out from participation in the favours of the crown. They now exulted in the near prospect of greatness and of vengeance. Burning with resentment, flushed with victory and hope, they would hear of no compromise. Nothing less than the deposition of their enemy would content them; nor can it be disputed that herein they were perfectly consistent. They had exerted themselves, nine years earlier, to exclude him from the throne, because they thought it likely that he would be a bad King. It could therefore scarcely be expected that they would willingly leave him on the throne, now that he had turned out a far worse King than any reasonable man could have anticipated.

On the other hand, not a few of William's followers were zealous Tories, who had, till very recently, held the doctrine of nonresistance in the most absolute form, but whose faith in that doctrine had, for a moment, given way to the strong passion excited by the ingratitude of the King and by the peril of the Church. No situation could be more painful or perplexing than that of the old Cavalier who found himself in arms against the throne. The scruples which had not prevented him from repairing to the Dutch camp began to torment him cruelly as soon as he was there. His mind misgave him that he had committed a crime. At all events he had exposed himself to reproach, by acting in diametrical opposition to the professions of his whole life. He felt insurmountable disgust for his new allies. They were people whom, ever since he could remember, he had been reviling and persecuting, Presbyterians, Independents, Anabaptists, old soldiers of Cromwell, brisk boys of Shaftesbury, accomplices in the Rye House plot, captains of the Western insurrection. He naturally wished to find out some salvo which might soothe his conscience, which might vindicate his consistency, and which might put a distinction between him and the crew of schismatical rebels whom he had always despised and abhorred, but with whom he was now in danger of being confounded. He therefore disclaimed with vehemence all thought of taking the crown from that anointed head which the ordinance of heaven and the fundamental laws of the realm had made sacred. His dearest wish was to see a reconciliation effected on terms which would not lower the royal dignity. He was no traitor. He was not, in truth, resisting the kingly authority. He was in arms only because he was convinced that the best service which could be rendered to the throne was to rescue His Majesty, by a little gentle coercion, from the hands of wicked counsellors.

The evils which the mutual animosity of these factions tended to produce were, to a great extent, averted by the ascendancy and by the wisdom of the Prince. Surrounded by eager disputants, officious advisers, abject flatterers, vigilant spies, malicious talebearers, he remained serene and inscrutable. He preserved silence while silence was possible. When he was forced to speak, the earnest and peremptory tone in which he uttered his well weighed opinions soon silenced everybody else. Whatever some of his too zealous adherents might say, he uttered not a word indicating any design on the English crown. He was doubtless well aware that between him and that crown were still interposed obstacles which no prudence might be able to surmount, and which a single false step would make insurmountable. His only chance of obtaining the splendid prize was not to seize it rudely, but to wait till, without any appearance of exertion or stratagem on his part, his secret wish should be accomplished by the force of circumstances, by the blunders of his opponents, and by the free choice of the Estates of the Realm. Those who ventured to interrogate him learned nothing, and yet could not accuse him of shuffling. He quietly referred them to his Declaration, and assured them that his views had undergone no change since that instrument had been drawn up.

James sent commissioners to Hungerford to negotiate with William, but used the negotiations to gain time to prepare for his own flight, which was also what William and his Whig followers most wanted. Only Tories, torn between their anxiety for the Church of England confronted by the King's aggressive Catholicism, and their adherence to the principle that monarchs could never be rightfully deposed, wanted them to succeed. James' flight made their position untenable and relieved William of serious embarrassment.

It seems probable that, even in the extremity to which [James] was now reduced, all his enemies united would have been unable to effect his complete overthrow had he not been his own worst enemy: but while his Commissioners were labouring to save him, he was labouring as earnestly to make all their efforts useless.

His plans were at length ripe for execution. The pretended negotiations had answered its purpose. On the same day on which the three Lords reached Hungerford the Prince of Wales arrived at Westminster. It had been intended that he should come over London Bridge; and some Irish troops were sent to Southwark to meet him. But they were received by a great multitude with such hooting and execration that they thought it advisable to retire with all speed. The poor child crossed the Thames at Kingston, and was brought into Whitehall so privately that many believed him to be still at Portsmouth.

To send him and the Queen out of the country without delay was now the first object of James. But who could be trusted to manage the escape? Dartmouth was accounted the most loyal of Protestant Tories; and Dartmouth had refused. Dover was a creature of the Jesuits; and even Dover had hesitated. It was not very easy to find an Englishman of rank and honour who would undertake to place the heir apparent of the English crown in the hands of the King of France. In these circumstances James bethought him of a French nobleman who then resided in London, Antonine Count of Lauzun. Of this man it has been said that his life was stranger than the dreams of other people. At any early age he had been the intimate associate of Lewis, and had been encouraged to expect the highest employments under the French crown. Then his fortune had undergone an eclipse. Lewis had driven from him the friend of his youth with bitter reproaches, and had, it was said, scarcely refrained from adding blows. The

fallen favourite had been sent prisoner to a fortress; but
he had emerged from his confinement, had again enjoyed
the smiles of his master, and had gained the heart of one
of the greatest ladies in Europe, Anna Maria, daughter of
Gaston Duke of Orleans, grand-daughter of King Henry the
Fourth, and heiress of the immense domains of the house
of Montpensier. The lovers were bent on marriage. The
royal consent was obtained. During a few hours Lauzun was
regarded by the court as an adopted member of the house of
Bourbon. The portion which the princess brought with her
might well have been an object of competition to sovereigns;
three great dukedoms, an independent principality with its
own mint and with its own tribunals, and an income greatly
exceeding the whole revenue of the kingdom of Scotland.
But this splendid prospect had been overcast. The match had
been broken off. The aspiring suitor had been, during many
years, shut up in a remote castle. At length Lewis relented.
Lauzun was forbidden to appear in the royal presence, but
was allowed to enjoy liberty at a distance from the court. He
visited England, and was well received at the palace of James
and in the fashionable circles of London; for in that age the
gentlemen of France were regarded throughout Europe as
models of grace; and many Chevaliers and Viscounts who
had never been admitted to the interior circle at Versailles,
found themselves objects of general curiosity and admiration
at Whitehall. Lauzun was in every respect the man for the
present emergency. He had courage and a sense of honour,
had been accustomed to eccentric adventures, and, with the
keen observation and ironical pleasantry of a finished man of
the world, had a strong propensity to knight errantry. All his
national feelings and all his personal interests impelled him

to undertake the adventure from which the most devoted subjects of the English crown seemed to shrink. As the guardian, at a perilous crisis, of the Queen of Great Britain and of the Prince of Wales, he might return with honour to his native land: he might once more be admitted to see Lewis dress and dine, and might, after so many vicissitudes, recommence, in the decline of life, the strangely fascinating chase of royal favour.

Animated by such feelings, Lauzun eagerly accepted the high trust which was offered to him. The arrangements for the flight were promptly made: a vessel was ordered to be in readiness at Gravesend: but to reach Gravesend was not easy. The city was in a state of extreme agitation. The slightest cause sufficed to bring a crowd together. No foreigner could appear in the streets without risk of being stopped, questioned, and carried before a magistrate as a Jesuit in disguise. It was, therefore, necessary to take the road to the south of the Thames. No precaution which could quiet suspicion was omitted. The King and Queen retired to rest as usual. When the palace had been some time profoundly quiet, James rose and called a servant who was in attendance. "You will find," said the King, "a man at the door of the antechamber. Bring him hither." The servant obeyed, and Lauzun was ushered into the royal bedchamber. "I confide to you," said James, "my Queen and my son; everything must be risked to carry them into France." Lauzun, with a truly chivalrous spirit, returned thanks for the dangerous honour which had been conferred on him, and begged permission to avail himself of the assistance of his friend Saint Victor, a gentleman of Provence, whose courage and faith had been often tried. The services of so valuable an assistant were readily accepted. Lauzun gave his hand to Mary. Saint Victor wrapped up in his warm cloak the ill fated heir of so many Kings. The party stole down the back stairs, and embarked in an open skiff. It was a miserable voyage. The night was bleak: the rain fell: the wind roared: the water was rough: at length the boat reached Lambeth; and the fugitives landed near an inn, where a coach and horses were in waiting. Some time elapsed before the horses could be harnessed. Mary, afraid that her face might be known, would not enter the house. She remained with her child, cowering for shelter from the storm under the tower of Lambeth Church, and distracted by terror whenever the ostler approached her with his lantern. Two of her women attended her, one who gave suck to the Prince, and one whose office was to rock his cradle; but they could be of little use to their mistress; for both were foreigners who could hardly speak the English language, and who shuddered at the rigour of the English climate. The only consolatory circumstance was that the little boy was well, and uttered not a single cry. At length the coach was ready. Saint Victor followed it on horseback. The fugitives reached Gravesend safely, and embarked in the yacht which waited for them. They found there Lord Powis and his wife. Three Irish officers were also on board. These men had been sent thither in order that they might assist Lauzun in the desperate emergency; for it was thought not impossible that the captain of the ship might prove false; and it was fully determined that, on the first suspicion of treachery, he should be stabbed to the heart. There was, however, no necessity for violence. The yacht proceeded down the river with a fair wind; and Saint Victor, having seen her under sail, spurred back with the good news to Whitehall.

On the morning of Monday, the tenth of December, the King learned that his wife and son had begun their voyage with a fair prospect of reaching their destination. About the same time a courier arrived at the palace with despatches from Hungerford. Had James been a little more discerning, or a little less obstinate, those despatches would have induced him to reconsider all his plans. The Commissioners wrote hopefully. The conditions proposed by the conqueror were strangely liberal. The King himself could not refrain from exclaiming that they were more favourable than he could have expected. He might indeed not unreasonably suspect that they had been framed with no friendly design: but this mattered nothing; for, whether they were offered in the hope that, by closing with them, he would lay the ground for a happy reconciliation, or, as is more likely, in the hope that, by rejecting them, he would exhibit himself to the whole nation as utterly unreasonable and incorrigible, his course was equally clear. In either case his policy was to accept them promptly and to observe them faithfully.

But it soon appeared that William had perfectly understood the character with which he had to deal, and, in offering those terms which the Whigs at Hungerford had censured as too indulgent, had risked nothing. The solemn farce by which the public had been amused since the retreat of the royal army from Salisbury was prolonged during a few hours. All the Lords who were still in the capital were invited to the palace that they might be informed of the progress of the negotiation which had been opened by their advice. Another meeting of peers was appointed for the following day. The Lord Mayor and the Sheriffs of London were summoned to attend the King. He exhorted them to perform their duties vigorously, and owned that he had thought it expedient to send his wife and child out of the country, but assured them that he would himself remain at his post. While he uttered this unkingly and unmanly falsehood, his fixed purpose was to depart before daybreak. Already he had entrusted his most valuable movables to the care of several foreign Ambassadors. His most important papers had been deposited with the Tuscan minister. But before the flight there was still something to be done. The tyrant pleased himself with the thought that he might avenge himself on a people who had been impatient of his despotism by inflicting on them at parting all the evils of anarchy. He ordered the Great Seal and the writs for the new Parliament to be brought to his apartment. The writs he threw into the fire. Some which had been already sent out he annulled by an instrument drawn up in legal form. To Feversham[10] he wrote a letter which could be understood only as a command to disband the army. Still, however, he concealed, even from his chief ministers, his intention of absconding. Just before he retired he directed Jeffreys to be in the closet early on the morrow, and, while stepping into bed, whispered to Mulgrave that the news from Hungerford was highly satisfactory. Everybody withdrew except the Duke of Northumberland. This young man, a natural son of Charles the Second by the Duchess of Cleveland, commanded a troop of Life Guards, and was a Lord of the Bedchamber. It seems to have been then the custom of the court that, in the Queen's absence, a Lord of the Bedchamber should sleep on a pallet in the King's room; and it was Northumberland's turn to perform this duty.

At three in the morning of Tuesday the eleventh of December, James rose, took the Great Seal in his hand, laid his commands on Northumberland not to open the door of the bedchamber till the usual hour, and disappeared through a secret passage, the same passage probably through which Huddleston had been brought to the bedside of the late King. Sir Edward Hales was in attendance with a hackney coach. James was conveyed to Millbank, where he crossed the Thames in a small wherry. As he passed Lambeth he flung the Great Seal into the midst of the stream, where, after many months, it was accidentally caught by a fishing net and dragged up.

At Vauxhall he landed. A carriage and horses had been stationed there for him; and he immediately took the road towards Sheerness, where a hoy belonging to the Custom House had been ordered to await his arrival.

Northumberland strictly obeyed the injunction which had been laid on him, and did not open the door of the royal apartment till it was broad day. The antechamber was filled with courtiers who came to make their morning bow and with Lords who had been summoned to Council. The news of James's flight passed in an instant from the galleries to the streets; and the whole capital was in commotion.

It was a terrible moment. The King was gone. The Prince had not arrived. No Regency had been appointed. The Great Seal, essential to the administration of ordinary justice, had disappeared. It was soon known that Feversham had, on the receipt of the royal order, instantly disbanded his forces. What respect for law or property was likely to be found among soldiers, armed and congregated, emancipated from the restraints of discipline, and destitute of the necessaries of life? On the other hand, the populace of London had, during some weeks, shown a strong disposition to turbulence and rapine. The urgency of the crisis united for a short time all who had any interest in the peace of society. Rochester had till that day adhered firmly to the royal cause. He now saw that there was only one way of averting general confusion. "Muster your troop of Guards," he said to Northumberland; "and declare for the Prince of Orange." The advice was promptly followed. The principal officers of the army who were then in London held a meeting at Whitehall, and resolved that they would submit to William's authority, and would, till his pleasure should be known, keep their men together, and assist the civil power to preserve order.

Who was to supply, at that awful crisis, the place of the King? In the days of the Plantagenets, if a suspension of the regal functions took place, the Lords Spiritual and Temporal generally assumed the supreme executive power. It was by the Lords that provision was made for the government of the kingdom during the minority of Henry the Third and during the absence of Edward the First. Both when Henry the Sixth succeeded to the crown in his infancy, and when many years later he sank into imbecility, the Lords took upon themselves to administer the government in his stead till the legislature had appointed a Protector. Whether our old Barons and Prelates, in acting for a King who could not act for himself, exercised a strictly legal right, or committed an irregularity which only extreme necessity could excuse, is a question which has been much debated. But the morning of the eleventh of December 1688 was not a time for controversy. It was necessary to the public safety that there should be a provisional government; and the eyes of men naturally turned to the magnates of the realm. Most of the

Peers who were in the capital repaired to Guildhall, and were received there with all honour by the magistracy of the City. The extremity of the danger drew Sancroft forth from his palace. He took the chair; and, under his presidency, the new Archbishop of York, five Bishops, and twenty-two temporal Lords determined to draw up, subscribe, and publish a Declaration. By this instrument they declared that they were firmly attached to the religion and constitution of their country, and that they had cherished the hope of seeing grievances redressed and tranquillity restored by the Parliament which the King had lately summoned, but that this hope had been extinguished by his flight. They had therefore determined to join with the Prince of Orange, in order that the freedom of the nation might be vindicated, that the rights of the Church might be secured, that a just liberty of conscience might be given to Dissenters, and that the Protestant interest throughout the world might be strengthened. Till His Highness should arrive, they were prepared to take on themselves the responsibility of giving such directions as might be necessary for the preservation of order. A deputation was instantly sent to lay this Declaration before the Prince, and to inform him that he was impatiently expected in London.

The Lords then proceeded to deliberate on the course which it was necessary to take for the prevention of tumult. They sent for the two Secretaries of State. Middleton refused to submit to what he regarded as an illegitimate authority; but Preston, astounded by his master's flight, and not knowing what to expect, or whither to turn, obeyed the summons. A message was sent to Skelton, who was Lieutenant of the Tower, requesting his attendance at Guildhall. He came, and was told that his services were no longer wanted, and that he must instantly deliver up his keys. He was succeeded by Lord Lucas. At the same time the Peers ordered a letter to be written to Dartmouth, enjoining him to refrain from all hostile operations against the Dutch fleet, and to displace all the Popish officers who held commands under him.

The part taken in these proceedings by Sancroft, and by some other persons who had, up to that day, been strictly faithful to the principle of passive obedience, deserves especial notice. To usurp the command of the military and naval forces of the state, to remove the officers whom the King had set over his castles and his ships, and to prohibit his Admiral from giving battle in defence of the royal cause, was surely nothing less than rebellion. Yet several honest and able Tories of the school of Filmer persuaded themselves that they could do all these things without incurring the guilt of resisting their Sovereign. The distinction which they took was, at least, ingenious. Government, they said, is the ordinance of God. Hereditary monarchical government is eminently the ordinance of God. While the King commands what is lawful we must obey him actively. When he commands what is unlawful we must obey him passively. In no extremity are we justified in withstanding him by force. But if he chooses to resign his office, his rights over us are at an end. While he governs us, though he may govern us ill, we are bound to submit; but, if he refuses to govern us at all, we are not bound to remain for ever without a government. Anarchy is not the ordinance of God; nor will he impute it to us as a sin that, when a prince, whom, in spite of extreme provocations, we have never ceased to honour and obey, has departed we know not whither, leaving no vicegerent, we

117

take the only course which can prevent the entire dissolution of society. Had our Sovereign remained among us, we were ready, little as he deserved our love, to die at his feet. Had he, when he quitted us, appointed a regency to govern us with vicarious authority during his absence, to that regency alone should we have looked for direction. But he has disappeared, having made no provision for the preservation of order or the administration of justice. With him, and with his Great Seal, has vanished the whole machinery by which a murderer can be punished, by which the right to an estate can be decided, by which the effects of a bankrupt can be distributed. His last act has been to free thousands of armed men from the restraints of military discipline, and to place them in such a situation that they must plunder or starve. Yet a few hours, and every man's hand will be against his neighbour. Life, property, female honour, will be at the mercy of every lawless spirit. We are at this moment actually in that state of nature about which theorists have written so much; and in that state we have been placed, not by our fault, but by the voluntary defection of him who ought to have been our protector. His defection may be justly called voluntary: for neither his life nor his liberty was in danger. His enemies had just consented to treat with him on a daily basis proposed by himself, and had offered immediately to suspend all hostile operations, on conditions which he could not deny to be liberal. In such circumstances it is that he has abandoned his trust. We retract nothing. We are in nothing inconsistent. We still assert our old doctrines without qualification. We still hold that it is in all cases sinful to resist the magistrate; but we say that there is no longer any magistrate to resist. He who was the magistrate, after long abusing his powers, has at last abdicated them. The abuse did not give us a right to consider how we may best supply his place.

It was on these grounds that the Prince's party was now swollen by many adherents who had previously stood aloof from it. Never, within the memory of man, had there been so near an approach to entire concord among all intelligent Englishmen as at this conjuncture; and never had concord been more needed. All those evil passions which it is the office of government to restrain, and which the best governments restrain but imperfectly, were on a sudden emancipated from control; avarice, licentiousness, revenge, the hatred of sect to sect, the hatred of nation to nation. On such occasions it will ever be found that the human vermin, which, neglected by ministers of state, and ministers of religion, barbarous in the midst of civilisation, heathen in the midst of Christianity, burrows, among all physical and all moral pollution, in the cellars and garrets of great cities, will at once rise into a terrible importance. So it was now in London. When the night, the longest night, as it chanced, of the year approached, forth came from every den of vice, from the bear garden at Hockley, and from the labyrinth of tippling houses and brothels in the Friars, thousands of housebreakers and highwaymen, cutpurses and ringdroppers. With these were mingled thousands of idle apprentices, who wished merely for the excitement of a riot. Even men of peaceable and honest habits were impelled by religious animosity to join the lawless part of the population. For the cry of No Popery, a cry which has more than once endangered the existence of London, was the signal for outrage and rapine. First the rabble fell on the Roman Catholic places of worship. The buildings were demolished. Benches, pulpits, confessionals, breviaries were heaped up and set on fire. A great mountain of books and furniture blazed on the site of the convent at Clerkenwell. Another pile was kindled before the ruins of the Franciscan house in Lincoln's Inn Fields. The chapel in Lime Street, the chapel in Bucklersbury, were pulled down. The pictures, images, and crucifixes were carried along the streets in triumph, amidst lighted tapers torn from the altars. The procession bristled thick with swords and staves, and on the point of every sword and of every staff was an orange. The King's printing house, whence had issued, during the preceding three years, innumerable tracts in defence of Papal supremacy, image worship, and monastic vows, was – to use a coarse metaphor which then, for the first time, came into fashion – completely gutted. The vast stock of paper, much of which was still unpolluted by types, furnished an immense bonfire. From monasteries, temples, and public offices, the fury of the multitude turned to private dwellings. Several houses were pillaged and destroyed: but the smallness of the booty disappointed the plunderers; and soon a rumour was spread that the most valuable effects of the Papists had been placed under the care of the foreign Ambassadors. To the savage and ignorant populace the law of nations and the risk of bringing on their country the just vengeance of all Europe were as nothing. The houses of the Ambassadors were besieged. A great crowd assembled before Barillon's door in St. James's Square. He, however, fared better than might have been expected. For, though the government which he represented was held in abhorrence, his liberal housekeeping and exact payments had made him personally popular. Moreover he had taken the precaution of asking for a guard of soldiers; and, as several men of rank, who lived near him had done the same, a considerable force was collected in their square. The rioters, therefore, when they were assured that no arms or priests were concealed under his roof, left him unmolested. The Venetian Envoy was protected by a detachment of troops: but the mansions occupied by the ministers of the Elector Palatine and of the Grand Duke of Tuscany were destroyed. One precious box the Tuscan minister was able to save from the marauders. It contained nine volumes of memoirs, written in the hand of James himself. These volumes reached France in safety, and, after the lapse of more than a century, perished there in the havoc of a revolution far more terrible than that from which they had escaped. But some fragments still remain, and, though grievously mutilated, and imbedded in masses of childish fiction, well deserve to be attentively studied.

The rich plate of the Chapel Royal had been deposited at Wild House, near Lincoln's Inn Fields, the residence of the Spanish ambassador Ronquillo. Ronquillo, conscious that he and his court had not deserved ill of the English nation, had thought it unnecessary to ask for soldiers: but the mob was not in a mood to make nice distinctions. The name of Spain had long been associated in the public mind with the Inquisition and the Armada, with the cruelties of Mary and the plots against Elizabeth. Ronquillo had also made himself many enemies among the common people by availing himself of his privilege to avoid the necessity of paying his debts. His house was therefore sacked without mercy; and a noble library, which he had collected, perished in the flames. His only comfort was that the host in his chapel was rescued from the same fate.

The morning of the twelfth of December rose on a ghastly

sight. The capital in many places presented the aspect of a city taken by storm. The Lords met at Whitehall, and exerted themselves to restore tranquillity. The trainbands were ordered under arms. A body of cavalry was kept in readiness to disperse tumultuous assemblages. Such atonement as was at that moment possible was made for the gross insults which had been offered to foreign governments. A reward was promised for the discovery of the property taken from Wild House; and Ronquillo, who had not a bed or an ounce of plate left, was splendidly lodged in the deserted palace of the Kings of England. A sumptuous table was kept for him; and the yeomen of the guard were ordered to wait in his antechamber with the same observance which they were in the habit of paying to the Sovereign. These marks of respect soothed even the punctilious pride of the Spanish court, and averted all danger of a rupture.

In spite, however, of the well meant efforts of a provisional government, the agitation grew hourly more formidable. It was heightened by an event which, even at this distance of time, can hardly be related without a feeling of vindictive pleasure. A scrivener who lived at Wapping, and whose trade was to furnish the seafaring men there with money at high interest, had some time before lent a sum on bottomry. The debtor applied to equity for relief against his own bond; and the case came before Jeffreys. The counsel for the borrower, having little else to say, said that the lender was a Trimmer. The Chancellor instantly fired. "A Trimmer! where is he? Let me see him. I have heard of that kind of monster. What is it made like?" The unfortunate creditor was forced to stand forth. The Chancellor glared fiercely on him, stormed at him, and sent him away half dead with fright. "While I live," the poor man said, as he tottered out of the court, "I shall never forget that terrible countenance." And now the day of retribution had arrived. The Trimmer was walking through Wapping, when he saw a well known face looking out of the window of an alehouse. He could not be deceived. The eyebrows, indeed had been shaved away. The dress was that of a common sailor from Newcastle, and was black with coal dust: but there was no mistaking the savage eye and mouth of Jeffreys. The alarm was given. In a moment the house was surrounded by hundreds of people shaking bludgeons and bellowing curses. The fugitive's life was saved by a company of the trainbands; and he was carried before the Lord Mayor. The Mayor was a simple man who had passed his whole life in obscurity, and was bewildered by finding himself an important actor in a mighty revolution. The events of the last twenty-four hours, and the perilous state of the city which was under his charge, had disordered his mind and his body. When the great man, at whose frown, a few days before, the whole kingdom had trembled, was dragged into the justice room begrimed with ashes, half dead with fright, and followed by a raging multitude, the agitation of the unfortunate Mayor rose to the height. He fell into fits, and was carried to his bed, whence he never rose. Meanwhile the throng without was constantly becoming more numerous and more savage. Jeffreys begged to be sent to prison. An order to that effect was procured from the Lords who were sitting at Whitehall; and he was conveyed in a carriage to the Tower. Two regiments of militia were drawn out to escort him, and found the duty a difficult one. It was repeatedly necessary for them to form, as if for the purpose of repelling a charge of cavalry, and to present a forest of pikes to the mob. The thousands who were disappointed of their revenge pursued to coach, with howls of rage, to the gates of the Tower, brandishing cudgels, and holding up halters full in the prisoner's view. The wretched man meantime was in convulsions of terror. He wrung his hands: he looked wildly out, sometimes at one window, sometimes at the other, and was heard even above the tumult, crying "Keep them off, gentlemen! For God's sake keep them off!" At length, having suffered far more than the bitterness of death, he was safely lodged in the fortress where some of his most illustrious victims had passed their last days, and where his own life was destined to close in unspeakable ignominy and horror.

All this time an active search was making after Roman Catholic priests. Many were arrested. Two Bishops, Ellis and Leyburn, were sent to Newgate. The Nuncio, who had little reason to expect that either his spiritual or his political character would be respected by the multitude, made his escape, disguised as a lacquey, in the train of the minister of the Duke of Savoy.

Another day of agitation and alarm closed, and was followed by a night the strangest and most terrible that England had ever seen. Early in the evening an attack was made by the rabble on a stately house which had been built a few months before for Lord Powis, which, in the reign of George the Second, was the residence of the Duke of Newcastle, and which is still conspicuous at the northwestern angle of Lincoln's Inn Fields. Some troops were sent thither: the mob was dispersed, tranquillity seemed to be restored, and the citizens were retiring quietly to their beds. Just at this time arose a whisper which swelled fast into a fearful clamour, passed in an hour from Piccadilly to Whitechapel, and spread into every street and alley of the capital. It was said that the Irish whom Feversham had let loose were marching on London and massacring every man, woman, and child on the road. At one in the morning the drums of the militia beat to arms. Everywhere terrified women were weeping and wringing their hands, while their fathers and husbands were equipping themselves for fight. Before two the capital wore a face of stern preparedness which might well have daunted a real enemy, if such an enemy had been approaching. Candles were blazing at all the windows. The public places were as bright as at noonday. All the great avenues were barricaded. More than twenty thousand pikes and muskets lined the streets. The late daybreak of the winter solstice found the whole City still in arms. During many years the Londoners retained a vivid recollection of what they called the Irish night. When it was known that there had been no danger, attempts were made to discover the origin of the rumour which had produced so much agitation. It appeared that some persons who had the look and dress of clowns just arrived from the country had first spread the report in the suburbs a little before midnight: but whence these men came, and by whom they were employed, remained a mystery. And soon news arrived from many quarters which bewildered the public mind still more. The panic had not been confined to London. The cry that disbanded Irish soldiers were coming to murder the Protestants had, with malignant ingenuity, been raised at once in many places widely distant from each other. Great numbers of letters, skilfully framed for the purpose of frightening ignorant people, had been sent by stage coaches, by waggons, and by the post, to various parts of England. All these letters came to hand almost at the same time. In a hundred towns at once the populace was possessed with the belief that armed barbarians were at hand, bent on perpetrating crimes as foul as those which had disgraced the rebellion of Ulster. No Protestant could find mercy. Children would be compelled by torture to murder their parents. Babes would be stuck on pikes, or flung into the blazing ruins of what had lately been happy dwellings. Great multitudes assembled with weapons: the people in some places began to pull down bridges, and to throw up barricades: but soon the excitement went down. In many districts those who had been so foully imposed upon learned with delight, alloyed by shame, that there was not a single Popish soldier within a week's march. There were places, indeed, where some straggling bands of Irish made their appearance and demanded food: but it can scarcely be imputed to them as a crime that they did not choose to die of hunger; and there is no evidence that they committed any wanton outrage. In truth they were much less numerous than was commonly supposed; and their spirit was cowed by finding themselves left on a sudden, without leaders or provisions, in the midst of a mighty population which felt towards them as men feel towards a drove of wolves. Of all the subjects of James none had more reason to execrate him than these unfortunate members of his church and defenders of his throne.

It is honourable to the English character that, notwith-standing the aversion with which the Roman Catholic religion and the Irish race were then regarded, notwithstanding the anarchy which was the effect of the flight of James, notwithstanding the artful machinations where were employed to scare the multitude into cruelty, no atrocious crime was perpetrated at this conjuncture. Much property, indeed, was destroyed and carried away. The houses of many Roman Catholic gentlemen were attacked. Parks were ravaged. Deer were slain and stolen. Some venerable specimens of the domestic architecture of the middles ages bear to this day the marks of the popular violence. The roads were in many places made impassable by a selfappointed police, which stopped every traveller till he proved that he was not a Papist. The Thames was infested by a set of pirates who, under pretence of searching for arms or delinquents, rummaged every boat that passed. Obnoxious persons were insulted and hustled. Many persons who were not obnoxious were glad to ransom their persons and effects by bestowing some guineas on the zealous Protestants who had, without any legal authority, assumed the office of inquisitors. But in all this confusion, which lasted several days and extended over many countries, not a single Roman Catholic lost his life. The mob showed no inclination to blood, except in the case of Jeffreys; and the hatred which that bad man inspired had more affinity with humanity than with cruelty.

At London William was impatiently expected: for it was not doubted that his vigour and ability would speedily restore order and security. There was however some delay for which the Prince cannot justly be blamed. His original intention had been to proceed from Hungerford to Oxford, where he was assured of an honourable and affectionate reception: but the arrival of the deputation from Guildhall induced him to change his intention and to hasten directly towards the capital. On the way he learned that Feversham, in pursuance of the King's orders, had dismissed the royal army, and that thousands of soldiers, freed from restraint and destitute of necessaries, were scattered over the counties through which the road to London lay. It was therefore impossible for William to proceed slenderly attended without great danger, not only in his own person, about which he was not much in the habit of being solicitous, but also to the great interests which were under his care. It was necessary that he should regulate his own movements by the movements of his troops; and troops could then move but slowly along the highways of England in midwinter. He was, on this occasion, a little moved from his ordinary composure. "I am not to be thus dealt with," he exclaimed with bitterness; "and that my Lord Feversham shall find." Prompt and judicious measures were taken to remedy the evils which James had caused. Churchill and Grafton were entrusted with the task of reassembling the dispersed army and bringing it into order. The English soldiers were invited to resume their military character. The Irish were commanded to deliver up their arms on pain of being treated as banditti, but were assured that, if they would submit quietly, they should be supplied with necessaries.

James was apprehended and brought back against William's wishes, but he was given ample opportunity to flee again, which he duly took advantage of, and William's troops were installed in London.

There could be no royal writ of summons of a Parliament, but the House of Lords was assembled. William invited members of Parliament who had sat in the Commons in Charles II's reign to assemble, James' recent House of Commons being regarded as having been packed and therefore ineligible. The two Houses called on William to summon a Convention, while William headed a temporary executive administration. Tories were divided over the essential constitutional question, a significant number favouring a Regency for James' infant son, while James continued to reign but not to rule; others put forward the notion that James by his flight had in effect abdicated. Whigs, however, as Macaulay says, found no difficulty in the idea of an alteration of the succession by Act of Parliament.

On the twenty-eighth of January the Commons resolved themselves into a Committee of the whole House. A member who had, more than thirty years before, been one of Cromwell's Lords, Richard Hampden, son of the illustrious man who had, by large bribes and degrading submissions, narrowly escaped with life from the vengeance of James, was placed in the chair, and the great debate began.

It was soon evident that an overwhelming majority considered James as no longer King. Gilbert Dolben, son of a late Archbishop of York, was the first who declared himself to be of that opinion. He was supported by many members, particularly by the bold and vehement Wharton, by Sawyer, whose stead opposition to the dispensing power had, in some measure, atoned for old offences, by Maynard, whose voice, though so feeble with age that it could not be heard on distant benches, still commanded the respect of all parties, and by Somers, whose luminous eloquence and varied stores of knowledge were on that day exhibited, for the first time, within the walls of Parliament. The unblushing forehead and voluble tongue of Sir William Williams were found on the same side. Already he had been deeply concerned in the excesses both of the worst of oppositions and of the worst of governments. He had persecuted innocent Papists and innocent Protestants. He had been the patron of Oates and the tool of Petre. His name was associated with seditious violence which was remembered with regret and shame by all respectable Whigs, and with freaks of despotism abhorred by all respectable Tories. How men live under such infamy is not easy to understand: but even such infamy was not enough for Williams. He was not ashamed to attack the fallen master to whom he had hired himself out for work which no honest man in the Inns of Court would undertake, and from whom he had, within six months, accepted a baronetcy as the reward of servility.

Only three members ventured to oppose themselves to what was evidently the general sense of the assembly. Sir Christopher Musgrave, a Tory gentleman of great weight and ability, hinted some doubts. Heneage Finch let fall some expressions which were understood to mean that he wished a negotiation to be opened with the King. This suggestion was so ill received that he made haste to explain it away. He protested that he had been misapprehended. He was convinced that, under such a prince, there could be no security for religion, liberty, or property. To recall King James, or to treat with him, would be a fatal course; but many who would never consent that he should exercise the regal power had conscientious scruples about depriving him of the royal title. There was one expedient which would remove all difficulties, a Regency. This proposition found so little favour that Finch did not venture to demand a division. Richard Fanshaw, Viscount Fanshaw of the kingdom of Ireland, said a few words in behalf of James, and recommended an adjournment; but the recommendation was met by a general outcry. Member after member stood up to represent the importance of despatch. Every moment, it was said, was precious: the public anxiety was intense: trade was suspended. The minority sullenly submitted, and suffered the predominant party to take its own course.

What that course would be was not perfectly clear. For the majority was made up of two classes. One class consisted of eager and vehement Whigs, who, if they had been able to take their own course, would have given to the proceedings of the Convention a decidedly revolutionary character. The other class admitted that a revolution was necessary, but regarded it as a necessary evil, and wished to disguise it, as much as possible, under the show of legitimacy. The former class demanded a distinct recognition of the right of subjects to dethrone bad princes. The latter class desired to rid the country of one bad prince, without promulgating any doctrine which might be abused for the purpose of weakening the just and salutary authority of future monarchs. The former class dwelt chiefly on the King's misgovernment; the latter on his flight. The former class considered him as having forfeited his crown; the latter as having resigned it. It was not easy to draw up any form of words which would please all whose assent it was important to obtain; but at length, out of many suggestions offered from different quarters, a resolution was framed that gave general satisfaction. It was moved that King James the Second, having endeavoured to subvert the constitution of the kingdom by breaking the original contract between King and people, and, by the advice of Jesuits and other wicked persons, having violated the fundamental laws, and having withdrawn himself out of the kingdom, had abdicated the government, and that the throne had thereby become vacant.

This resolution has been many times subjected to criticism as minute and severe as was ever applied to any sentence written by man: and perhaps there never was a sentence written by man which would bear such criticism less. That a King by grossly abusing his power may forfeit it is true. That a King, who absconds without making any provision for the administration, and leaves his people in a state of anarchy, may, without any violent straining of language, be said to have abdicated his functions is also true. But no accurate writer would affirm that long continued misgovernment and desertion, added together, make up an act of abdication. It is evident too that the mention of the Jesuits and other evil advisers of James weakens, instead of strengthening, the case against him. For it is a well known maxim of English law that, when a king is mislead by pernicious counsel, his counsellors, and not himself, ought to be held accountable for his errors. It is idle, however, to examine these memorable words as we should examine a chapter of Aristotle or of Hobbes. Such words are to be considered, not as words, but as deeds. If they effect that which they are intended to effect, they are rational though they may be contradictory. If they fail of attaining their end, they are absurd, though they carry demonstration with them. Logic admits of no compromise. The essence of politics is compromise. It is therefore not strange that some of the most important and most useful political instruments in the world should be among the most illogical compositions that ever were penned. The object of Somers, of Maynard, and of the other eminent men who shaped this celebrated motion was, not to leave to posterity a model of definition and partition, but to make the restoration of a tyrant impossible and to place on the throne a sovereign under whom law and liberty might be secure. This object they attained by using language which, in a philosophical treatise, would justly be reprehended as inexact and confused. They cared little whether their major agreed with their conclusion, if the major secured two hundred votes, and the conclusion two hundred more. In fact the one beauty of the resolution is its inconsistency. There was a phrase for every subdivision of the majority. The mention of the original contract gratified the disciples of Sidney. The word abdication conciliated politicians of a more timid school. There were doubtless many fervent Protestants who were pleased with the censure cast on the Jesuits. To the real statesman the single important clause was that which declared the throne vacant; and, if that clause could be carried, he cared little by what preamble it might be introduced. The force which was thus united made all resistance hopeless. The motion was adopted by the Committee without a division. It was ordered that the report should be instantly made. Powle returned to the chair: the mace was laid on the table: Hampden brought up the resolution: the House instantly agreed to it, and ordered him to carry it to the Lords.

On the following morning the Lords assembled early. The benches both of the spiritual and of the temporal peers were crowded. Hampden appeared at the bar, and put the resolution of the Commons into the hands of Halifax. The Upper House then resolved itself into a Committee; and Danby took the chair.

The discussion was soon interrupted by the reappearance of Hampden with another message. The House resumed and was informed that the Commons had just voted it inconsistent with the safety and welfare of this Protestant nation to be governed by a Popish King. To this resolution, irreconcilable as it obviously was with the doctrine of indefeasible hereditary right, the Peers gave an immediate and unanimous assent. The principle which was thus affirmed has always, down to our own time, been held sacred by all Protestant statesmen, and has never been considered by any reasonable Roman Catholic as objectionable. If, indeed, our sovereigns were, like the Presidents of the United States, mere civil functionaries, it would not be easy to vindicate such a restriction. But the headship of the English Church is annexed to the English crown; and there is no intolerance in saying that a Church ought not to be subjected to a head who regards her as schismatical and heretical.

After this short interlude the Lords again went into committee. The Tories insisted that their plan should be discussed before the vote of the Commons which declared the throne vacant was considered. This was conceded to them; and the question was put whether a Regency, exercising kingly power during the life of James, in his name, would be the best expedient for preserving the laws and liberties of the nation?

The contest was long and animated. The chief speakers in favour of a Regency were Rochester and Nottingham. Halifax and Danby led the other side. The Primate, strange to say, did not make his appearance, though earnestly importuned by the Tory peers to place himself at their head. His absence drew on him many contumelious censures; nor have even his eulogists been able to find any explanation of it which raises his character. The plan of Regency was his own. He had, a few days before, in a paper written with his own hand, pronounced that plan to be clearly the best that could be adopted. The deliberations of the Lords who supported that plan had been carried on under his roof. His situation made it his clear duty to declare publicly what he thought. Nobody can suspect him of personal cowardice or of vulgar cupidity. It was probably from a nervous fear of doing wrong that, at this great conjuncture, he did nothing: but he should have known that, situated as he was, to do nothing was to do wrong. A man who is too scrupulous to take on himself a grave responsibility at an important crisis ought to be too scrupulous to accept the place of first minister of the Church and first peer of the Parliament.

It is not strange, however, that Sancroft's mind should have been ill at ease; for he could hardly be blind to the obvious truth that the scheme which he had recommended to his friends was utterly inconsistent with all that he and his brethren had been teaching during many years. That the King had a divine and indefeasible right to the regal power, and that the regal power, even when most grossly abused, could not, without sin, be resisted, was the doctrine in which the Anglican Church had long gloried. Did this doctrine then really mean only that the King had a divine and indefeasible right to have his effigy and name cut on a seal which was to be daily employed in despite of him for the purpose of commissioning his enemies to levy war on him, and of sending his friends to the gallows for obeying him? Did the whole duty of a good subject consist in using the word King? If so, Fairfax and Cromwell at Naseby had performed all the duty of good subjects. For Charles had been designated as King even by the generals who commanded against him. Nothing in the conduct of the Long Parliament had been more severely blamed by the Church than the ingenious device of using his name against himself. Every one of her ministers had been required to sign a declaration condemning as traitorous the fiction by which the authority of the sovereign had been separated from his person. Yet this traitorous fiction was now considered by the Primate and by many of his suffragans as the only basis on which they could, in strict conformity with Christian principles, erect a government.

The distinction which Sancroft had borrowed from the Roundheads of the preceding generation subverted from the foundation that system of politics which the Church and the Universities pretended to have learned from Saint Paul. The Holy Spirit, it had been a thousand times repeated, had commanded the Romans to be subject to Nero. The meaning of the precept now appeared to be only that the Romans were to call Nero Augustus. They were perfectly at liberty to chase him beyond the Euphrates, to leave him a pensioner on the bounty of the Parthians, to withstand him by force if he attempted to return, to punish all who aided him or corresponded with him, and to transfer the Tribunitian power and the Consular power, the Presidency of the Senate and the command of the Legions, to Galba or Vespasian.

The analogy which the Archbishop imagined that he had discovered between the case of a wrongheaded king and the case of a lunatic king will not bear a moment's examination. It was plain that James was not in that state of mind in which, if he had been a country gentleman or a merchant, any tribunal would have held him incapable of executing a contract or a will. He was of unsound mind only as all bad kings are of unsound mind; as Charles the First had been of unsound mind when he went to seize the five members; as Charles the Second had been of unsound mind when he concluded the treaty of Dover. If this sort of mental unsoundness did not justify subjects in withdrawing their obedience from princes, the plan of a Regency was evidently indefensible. If this sort of mental unsoundness did justify subjects in withdrawing their obedience from princes, the doctrine of non-resistance was completely given up; and all that any moderate Whig had ever contended for was fully admitted.

As to the oath of allegiance about which Sancroft and his disciples were so anxious, one thing at least is clear, that, whoever might be right, they were wrong. The Whigs held that, in the oath of allegiance, certain conditions were implied, that the King had violated these conditions, and that the oath had therefore lost its force. But, if the Whig doctrine were false, if the oath were still binding, could men of sense really believe that they escaped the guilt of perjury by voting for a Regency? Could they affirm that they bore true allegiance to James, while they were, in defiance of his protestations made before all Europe, authorising another person to receive the royal revenues, to summon and prorogue Parliaments, to create Dukes and Earls, to name Bishops and Judges, to pardon offenders, to command the forces of the state, and to conclude treaties with foreign powers? Had Pascal been able to find, in all the folios of the Jesuitical casuists, a sophism more contemptible than that which now, as it seemed, sufficed to quiet the consciences of the fathers of the Anglican Church.

Nothing could be more evident than that the plan of Regency could be defended only on Whig principles. Between the rational supporters of that plan and the majority of the House of Commons there could be no dispute as to the question of right. All that remained was a question of expediency. And would any statesman seriously contend that it was expedient to constitute a government with two heads, and to give to one of those heads regal power without regal dignity, and to the other regal dignity without regal power? It was notorious that such an arrangement, even when made necessary by the infancy or insanity of a prince, had serious disadvantages. That times of Regency were times of weakness, of trouble, and of disaster, was a truth proved by the whole history of England, of France, and of Scotland, and had almost become a proverb. Yet, in a case of infancy or of insanity, the King was at least passive. He could not actively counterwork the Regent. What was now proposed was that England should have two first magistrates, of ripe age and sound mind, waging with each other an irreconcilable war. It was absurd to talk of leaving James merely the kingly name, and depriving him of all the kingly power. For the name was a part of the power. The word King was a word of conjuration. It was associated in the minds of many Englishmen with the idea of a mysterious character derived from above, and in the minds of almost all Englishmen with the idea of legitimate and venerable authority. Surely, if the title carried with it such power, those who maintained that James ought to be deprived of all power could not deny that he ought to be deprived of the title.

And how long was the anomalous government planned by the genius of Sancroft to last? Every argument which could be urged for setting it up at all might be urged with equal force for retaining it to the end of time. If the boy who had been carried into France was really born of the Queen, he would hereafter inherit the divine and indefeasible right to be called King. The same right would very probably be transmitted from Papist to Papist through the whole of the eighteenth and nineteenth centuries. Both the Houses had unanimously resolved that England should not be governed by a Papist. It might well be, therefore, that, from generation to generation, Regents would continue to administer the government in the name of vagrant and mendicant Kings. There was no doubt that the Regents must be appointed by Parliament. The effect, therefore, of this contrivance, a contrivance intended to preserve unimpaired the sacred principle of hereditary monarchy, would be that the monarchy would become really elective.

Another unanswerable reason was urged against Sancroft's plan. There was in the statute book a law which had been passed soon after the close of the long and bloody contest between the Houses of York and Lancaster, and which had been framed for the purpose of averting calamities such as the alternate victories of those Houses had brought on the nobility and gentry of the realm. By this law it was provided that no person should, by adhering to a King in possession, incur the penalties of treason. When the regicides were brought to trail after the Restoration, some of them insisted that their case lay within the equity of this act. They had obeyed, they said, the government which was in possession, and were therefore not traitors. The Judges admitted that this would have been a good defence if the prisoners had acted under the authority of an usurper who, like Henry the Fourth and Richard the Third, bore the regal title, but declared that such a defence could not avail men who had indicted, sentenced, and executed one who, in the indictment, in the sentence, and in the death warrant, was designated as

King. It followed, therefore, that whoever should support a Regent in opposition to James would run great risk of being hanged, drawn and quartered, if ever James should recover supreme power; but that no person could, without such a violation of law as Jeffreys himself would hardly venture to commit, be punished for siding with a King who was reigning, though wrongfully, at Whitehall, against a rightful King who was in exile at Saint Germains.

It should seem that these arguments admit of no reply; and they were doubtless urged with force by Danby, who had a wonderful power of making every subject which he treated clear to the dullest mind, and by Halifax, who, in fertility of thought and brilliancy of diction, had no rival among the orators of that age. Yet so numerous and powerful were the Tories of the Upper House that, notwithstanding the weakness of their case, the defection of their leader, and the ability of their opponents, they very nearly carried the day. A hundred Lords divided. Forty-nine voted for a Regency, fifty-one against it. In the minority were the natural children of Charles, the brothers in law of James, the Dukes of Somerset and Ormond, the Archbishop of York and eleven Bishops. No prelate voted in the majority except Compton and Trelawney.

It was near nine in the evening before the House rose. The following day was the thirtieth of January, the anniversary of the death of Charles the First. The great body of the Anglican clergy had, during many years, thought it a sacred duty to inculcate on that day the doctrines of non-resistance and passive obedience. Their old sermons were now of little use; and many divines were even in doubt whether they could venture to read the whole Liturgy. The Lower House had declared that the throne was vacant. The Upper had not yet expressed any opinion. It was therefore not easy to decide whether the prayers for the sovereign ought to be read. Every officiating minister took his own course. In most of the churches of the capital the petitions for James were omitted: but at Saint Margaret's, Sharp, Dean of Norwich, who had been requested to preach before the Commons, not only read to their faces the whole service as it stood in the book, but, before his sermon, implored, in his own words, a blessing on the King, and towards the close of his discourse, declaimed against the Jesuitical doctrine that princes might lawfully be deposed by their subjects. The Speaker, that very afternoon, complained to the House of this affront. "You pass a vote one day," he said; "and on the next day it is contradicted from the pulpit in your own hearing." Sharp was strenuously defended by the Tories, and had friends even among the Whigs: for it was not forgotten that he had incurred serious danger in the evil times by the courage with which, in defiance of the royal injunction, he had preached against Popery. Sir Christopher Musgrave very ingeniously remarked that the House had not ordered the resolution which declared the throne vacant to be published. Sharp, therefore, was not only not bound to know anything of that resolution, but could not have taken notice of it without a breach of privilege for which he might have been called to the bar and reprimanded on his knees. The majority felt that it was not wise at that conjuncture to quarrel with the clergy; and the subject was suffered to drop.

While the Commons were discussing Sharp's sermon, the Lords had again gone into a Committee on the state of the nation, and had ordered the resolution which pronounced the throne vacant to be read clause by clause.

The first expression on which a debate arose was that which recognised the original contract between king and people. It was not to be expected that the Tory peers would suffer a phrase which contained the quintessence of Whiggism to pass unchallenged. A division took place; and it was determined by fifty-three votes to forty-six that the words should stand.

The severe censure passed by the Commons on the administration of James was next considered, and was approved without one dissentient voice. Some verbal objections were made to the proposition that James had abdicated the government. It was urged that he might more correctly be said to have deserted it. This amendment was adopted, it should seem, with scarcely any debate, and without a division. By this time it was late; and the Lords again adjourned.

Up to this moment the small body of peers which was under the guidance of Danby had acted in firm union with Halifax and the Whigs. The effect of this union had been that the plan of Regency had been rejected, and the doctrine of the original contract affirmed. The proposition that James had ceased to be King had been the rallying point of the two parties which had made up the majority. But from that point their path diverged. The next question to be decided was whether the throne was vacant; and this was a question not merely verbal, but of grave practical importance. If the throne was vacant, the Estates of the Realm might place William in it. If it was not vacant, he could succeed to it only after his wife, after Anne, and after Anne's posterity.

It was, according to the followers of Danby, an established maxim that our country could not be, even for a moment, without a rightful prince. The man might die; but the magistrate was immortal. The man might abdicate; but the magistrate was irremovable. If, these politicians said, we once admit that the throne is vacant, we admit that it is elective. The sovereign whom we may place on it will be a sovereign, not after the English, but after the Polish, fashion. Even if we choose the very person who would reign by right of birth, still that person will reign not by right of birth, but in virtue of our choice, and will take as a gift what ought to be regarded as an inheritance. That salutary reverence with which the blood royal and the order of primogeniture have hitherto been regarded will be greatly diminished. Still more serious will the evil be, if we not only fill the throne by election, but fill it with a prince who has doubtless the qualities of a great and good ruler, and who has wrought a wonderful deliverance for us, but who is not first nor even second in the order of succession. If we once say that merit, however eminent, shall be a title to the crown, we disturb the very foundations of our polity, and furnish a precedent of which every ambitious warrior or statesman who may have rendered any great service to the public will be tempted to avail himself. This danger we avoid if we logically follow out the principles of the constitution to their consequences. There has been a demise of the crown. At the instant of the demise the next heir became our lawful sovereign. We consider the Princess of Orange as next heir; and we hold that she ought, without any delay, to be proclaimed, what she already is, our Queen.

The Whigs answered that it was idle to apply ordinary rules to a country in a state of revolution, that the great question now depending was not to be decided by the saws of pedantic Templars, and that, if it were to be so decided, such saws might be quoted on one side as well as the other. If it were a legal maxim that the throne could never be vacant, it was also a legal maxim that a living man could have no heir. James was still living. How then could the Princess of Orange be his heir? The truth was that the laws of England had made full provision for the succession when the power of a sovereign and his natural life terminated together, but had made no provision for the very rare cases in which his power terminated before the close of his natural life; and with one of those very rare cases the Convention had now to deal. That James no longer filled the throne both Houses had pronounced. Neither common law nor statute law designated any person as entitled to fill the throne between his demise and his decease. It followed that the throne was vacant, and that the Houses might invite the Prince of Orange to fill it. That he was not next in order of birth was true: but this was no disadvantage: on the contrary, it was a positive recommendation. Hereditary monarchy was a good political institution, but was by no means more sacred than other good political institutions. Unfortunately, bigoted and servile theologians had turned it into a religious mystery, almost as awful and as incomprehensible as transubstantiation itself. To keep the institution, and yet to get rid of the abject and noxious superstitions with which it had of late years been associated and which had made it a curse instead of a blessing to society, ought to be the first object of English statesmen; and that object would be best attained by slightly deviating for a time from the general rule of descent, and then returning to it.

Many attempts were made to prevent an open breach

between the party of the Prince and the party of the Princess. A great meeting was held at the Earl of Devonshire's house, and the dispute was warm. Halifax was the chief speaker for William, Danby for Mary. Of the mind of Mary Danby knew nothing. She had been some time expected in London, but had been detained in Holland, first by masses of ice which had blocked up the rivers, and, when the thaw came, by strong westerly winds. Had she arrived earlier the dispute would probably have been at once quieted. Halifax on the other side had no authority to say anything in William's name. The Prince, true to his promise that he would leave the settlement of the government to the Convention, had maintained an impenetrable reserve, and had not suffered any word, look, or gesture, indicative either of satisfaction or of displeasure, to escape him. One of his countrymen, who had a large share of his confidence, had been invited to the meeting, and was earnestly pressed by the Peers to give them some information. He long excused himself. At last he so far yielded to their urgency as to say, "I can only guess at His Highness's mind. If you wish to know what I guess, I guess that he would not like to be his wife's gentleman usher; but I know nothing." "I know something now, however," said Danby. "I know enough, and too much." He then departed; and the assembly broke up.

On the thirty-first of January the debate which had terminated thus in private was publicly renewed in the House of Peers. That day had been fixed for the national thanksgiving. An office had been drawn up for the occasion by several Bishops, among whom were Ken and Sprat. It is perfectly free both from the adulation and from the malignity by which such compositions were in that age too often deformed, and sustains, better perhaps than any occasional service which

145

has been framed during two centuries, a comparison with that great model of chaste, lofty, and pathetic eloquence, the Book of Common Prayer. The Lords went in the morning to Westminster Abbey. The Commons had desired Burnet to preach before them at Saint Margaret's. He was not likely to fall into the same error which had been committed in the same place on the preceding day. His vigorous and animated discourse doubtless called forth the loud hums of his auditors. It was not only printed by command of the House, but was translated into French for the edification of foreign Protestants. The day closed with the festivities usual on such occasions. The whole town shone bright with fireworks and bonfires: the roar of guns and the pealing of bells lasted till the night was far spent: but, before the lights were extinct and the streets silent, an event had taken place which threw a damp on the public joy.

The Peers had repaired from the Abbey to their house, and had resumed the discussion on the state of the nation. The last words of the resolution of the Commons were taken into consideration; and it soon became clear that the majority was not disposed to assent to those words. To near fifty Lords who held that the regal title still belonged to James were now added seven or eight who held that it had already devolved on Mary. The Whigs, finding themselves outnumbered, tried to compromise the dispute. They proposed to omit the words which pronounced the throne vacant, and simply to declare the Prince and Princess King and Queen. It was manifest that such a declaration implied, though it did not expressly affirm, all that the Tories were unwilling to concede. For nobody could pretend that William had succeeded to the regal office by right of birth. To pass a resolution acknowledging him as King was therefore an act of election; and how could there be an election without a vacancy? The proposition of the Whig Lords was rejected by fifty-two votes to forty-seven. The question was then put whether the throne was vacant. The Contents were only forty-one: the Noncontents fifty-five. Of the minority thirty-six protested.

During the two following days London was in an unquiet and anxious state. The Tories began to hope that they might be able again to bring forward their favourite plan of Regency with better success. Perhaps the Prince himself, when he found that he had no chance of wearing the crown, might prefer Sancroft's scheme to Danby's. It was better doubtless to be a King than to be a Regent: but it was better to be a Regent than to be a gentleman usher. On the other side the lower and fiercer class of Whigs, the old emissaries of Shaftesbury, the old associates of College, began to stir in the City. Crowds assembled in Palace Yard, and held threatening language. Lord Lovelace, who was suspected of having encouraged these assemblages, informed the Peers that he was charged with a petition requesting them instantly to declare the Prince and Princess of Orange King and Queen. He was asked by whom the petition was signed. "There are no hands to it yet," he answered; "but, when I bring it here next, there shall be hands enough." This menace alarmed and disgusted his own party. The leading Whigs were, in truth, even more anxious than the Tories that the deliberations of the Convention should be perfectly free, and that it should not be in the power of any adherent of James to allege that either House had acted under force. A petition, similar to that which had been entrusted to Lovelace, was brought into the House of Commons, but was contemptuously rejected. Maynard was foremost in protesting against the attempt of the rabble in the streets to overawe the Estates of the Realm. William sent for Lovelace, expostulated with him strongly, and ordered the magistrates to act with all vigour against all unlawful assemblies. Nothing in the history of our revolution is more deserving of admiration and of imitation than the manner in which the two parties in the Convention, at the very moment at which their disputes ran highest, joined like one man to resist the dictation of the mob of the capital.

But, though the Whigs were fully determined to maintain order and to respect the freedom of debate, they were equally determined to make no concession. On Saturday, the second of February, the Commons, without a division, resolved to adhere to their resolution as it originally stood. James, as usual, came to the help of his enemies. A letter from him to the Convention had just arrived in London. It had been transmitted to Preston by the apostate Melfort,[11] who was now high in favour at Saint Germains. The name of Melfort was an abomination to every Churchman. That he was still a confidential minister was alone sufficient to prove that his master's folly and perverseness were incurable. No member of either House ventured to propose that a paper which came from such a quarter should be read. The contents, however, were well known to all the town. His Majesty exhorted the Lords and Commons not to despair of his clemency, and graciously assured them that he would pardon those who had betrayed him, some few excepted, whom he did not name. How was it possible to do anything for a prince who, vanquished, deserted, banished, living on alms, told those who were the arbiters of his fate that, if they would set him on his throne again, he would hang only a few of them?

The contest between the two branches of the legislature lasted some days longer. On Monday, the fourth of February, the Peers resolved that they would insist on their amendments: but a protest to which thirty-nine names were subscribed was entered on the journals. On the following day the Tories determined to try their strength in the Lower House. They mustered there in great force. A motion was made to agree to the amendments of the Lords. Those who were for the plan of Sancroft and those who were for the plan of Danby divided together; but they were beaten by two hundred and eighty-two votes to a hundred and fifty-one. The House then resolved to request a free conference with the Lords.

At the same time strenuous efforts were making without the walls of Parliament to bring the dispute between the two branches of the legislature to a close. Burnet thought that the importance of the crisis justified him in publishing the great secret which the Princess had confided in him. He knew, he said, from her own lips, that it had long been her full determination, even if she came to the throne in the regular course of descent, to surrender her power, with the sanction of Parliament, into the hands of her husband. Danby received from her an earnest, and almost angry reprimand. She was, she wrote, the Prince's wife; she had no other wish than to be subject to him: the most cruel injury that could be done to her would be to set her up as his competitor; and she never could regard any person who took such a course as her true friend. The Tories had still one hope. Anne might insist on her own rights, and on those of her children. No effort was spared to stimulate her ambition, and to alarm her conscience. Her uncle Clarendon was especially active. A few weeks only had elapsed since the hope of wealth and greatness had impelled him to belie the boastful professions of his whole life, to desert the royal cause, to join with the Wildmans and the Fergusons, nay, to propose that the King should be sent a prisoner to a foreign land and immured in a fortress begirt by pestilential marshes. The lure which had produced this strange transformation was the Viceroyalty of Ireland. Soon, however, it appeared that the proselyte had little chance of obtaining the splendid prize on which his heart was set. He found that others were consulted on Irish affairs. His advice was never asked, and, when obtrusively and importunately offered, was coldly received. He repaired many times to Saint James's palace, but could scarcely obtain a word or a look. One day the Prince was writing: another day he wanted fresh air and must ride in the Park: on a third he was closeted with officers on military business and could see nobody. Clarendon saw that he was not likely to gain anything by the sacrifice of his principles, and determined to take them back again. In December ambition had converted him into a rebel. In January disappointment reconverted him into a Royalist. The uneasy consciousness that he had not been a consistent Tory gave a peculiar acrimony to his Toryism. In the House of Lords he had done all in his power to prevent a settlement. He now exerted, for the same end, all his influence over the Princess Anne. But his influence over her was small indeed when compared with that of the Churchills, who wisely called to their help two powerful allies, Tillotson, who, as a spiritual director, had, at that time, immense authority, and Lady Russell, whose noble and gentle virtues, proved by the most cruel of all trials, had gained for her the reputation of a saint. The Princess of Denmark, it was soon known, was willing that William should reign for life; and it was evident that to defend the cause of the daughters of James against themselves was a hopeless task.

And now William thought that the time had come when he ought to explain himself. He accordingly sent for Halifax, Danby, Shrewsbury, and some other political leaders of great note, and with that air of stoical apathy under which he had, from a boy, been in the habit of concealing his strongest emotions, addressed to them a few deeply meditated and weighty words.

He had hitherto, he said, remained silent: he had used neither solicitation nor menace: he had not even suffered a hint of his opinions or wishes to get abroad: but a crisis had now arrived at which it was necessary for him to declare his intentions. He had no right and no wish to dictate to the Convention. All that he claimed was the privilege of declining any office which he felt that he could not hold with honour to himself and with benefit to the public.

A strong party was for a Regency. It was for the Houses to determine whether such an arrangement would be for the interest of the nation. He had a decided opinion on that point; and he thought it right to say distinctly that he would not be Regent.

Another party was for placing the Princess on the throne and for giving to him, during her life, the title of King, and such a share in the administration as she might be pleased to allow him. He could not stoop to such a post. He esteemed the Princess in as much as it was possible for man to esteem woman: but not even from her would he accept a subordinate and a precarious place in the government. He was so made that he could not submit to be tied to the apron strings even of the best of wives. He did not desire to take any part in English affairs; but, if he did consent to take a part, there was one part only which he could usefully or honourably take. If the Estates offered him the crown for life, he would accept it. If not, he should, without repining, return to his native country. He concluded by saying that he thought it reasonable that the Lady Anne and her posterity should be preferred in the succession to any children whom he might have by any other wife than the Lady Mary.

The meeting broke up; and what the Prince had said was in a few hours known all over London. That he must be King was now clear. The only question was whether he should hold the regal dignity alone or conjointly with the Princess. Halifax and a few other politicians, who saw in a strong light the danger of dividing the supreme executive authority, thought it desirable that, during William's life, Mary should be only Queen Consort and a subject. But this arrangement, though much might doubtless be said for it in argument, shocked the general feeling even of those Englishmen who were most attached to the Prince. His wife had given an unprecedented proof of conjugal submission and affection; and the very least return that could be made to her would be to bestow on her the dignity of Queen Regnant. William Harbord, one of the most zealous of the Prince's adherents, was so much exasperated that he sprang out of the bed to which he was confined with gout, and vehemently declared that he never would have drawn a sword in His Highness's cause if he had foreseen that so shameful an arrangement would be made. No person took the matter up so eagerly as Burnet. His blood boiled at the wrong done to his kind patroness. He expostulated vehemently with Bentinck, and begged to be permitted to resign the chaplainship. "While I am His Highness's servant," said the brave and honest divine, "it would be unseemly in me to oppose any plan which may have his countenance. I therefore desire to be set free, that I may fight the Princess's battle with every faculty that God has given me." Bentinck prevailed on Burnet to defer an open declaration of hostilities till William's resolution should be distinctly known. In a few hours the scheme which had excited so much resentment was entirely given up; and all those who considered James as no longer King were agreed as to the way in which the throne must be filled. William and Mary must be King and Queen. The heads of both must appear together on the coin: writs must run in the names of both: both must enjoy all the personal dignities and immunities of royalty: but the administration, which could not be safely divided, must belong to William alone.

An now the time arrived for the free conference between the Houses. The managers for the Lords, in their robes, took their seats along one side of the table in the Painted Chamber: but the crowd of members of the House of Commons on the other side was so great that the gentlemen who were to argue the question in vain tried to get through. It was not without much difficulty and long delay that the Serjeant at Arms was able to clear a passage.

At length the discussion began. A full report of the speeches on both sides has come down to us. There are few students of history who have not taken up that report with eager curiosity and laid it down with disappointment. The question between the Houses was argued on both sides as a question of law. The objections which the Lords made to the resolution of the Commons were verbal and technical, and were met by verbal and technical answers. Somers vindicated the use of the word abdication by quotations from Grotius and Brissonius, Spigelius and Bartolus. When he was challenged to show any authority for the proposition that England could be without a sovereign, he produced the Parliament roll of the year 1399, in which it was expressly set forth that the kingly office was vacant during the interval between the resignation of Richard the Second and the enthroning of Henry the Fourth. The Lords replied by producing the Parliament roll of the first year of Edward the Fourth, from which it appeared that the record of 1399 had been solemnly annulled. They therefore maintained that the precedent on which Somers relied was no longer valid. Treby then came to Somers's assistance, and laid on the table the Parliament roll of the first year of Henry the Seventh, which repealed the act of Edward the Fourth, and consequently restore the validity of the record of 1399. After a colloquy of several hours the disputants separated. The Lords assembled in their own house. It was well understood that they were about to yield, and that the conference had been a mere form. The friends of Mary who found that, by setting her up as her husband's rival, they had deeply displeased her. Some of the Peers who had formerly voted for a Regency had determined to absent themselves or to support the resolution of the Lower House. Their opinion, they said, was unchanged; but any government was better than no government; and the country could not bear a prolongation of this agony of suspense. Even Nottingham, who, in the Painted Chamber, had taken the lead against the Commons, declared that, though his own conscience would not suffer him to give way, he was glad that the consciences of other men were less squeamish. Several Lords who had not yet voted in the Convention had been induced to attend; Lord Lexington, who had just hurried over from the Continent; the Earl of Lincoln, who was half mad; the Earl of Carlisle, who limped in on crutches; and the Bishop of Durham, who had been in hiding and had intended to fly beyond sea, but had received an intimation that, if he would vote for the settling of the government, his conduct in the Ecclesiastical Commission should not be remembered against him. Danby, desirous to heal the schism which he had caused, exhorted the House, in a speech distinguished by even more than his usual ability, not to persevere in a contest which might be fatal to the state. He was strenuously supported by Halifax. The spirit of the opposite party was quelled. When the question was put whether King James had abdicated the government, only three Lords said Not Content. On the question whether the throne was vacant, a division was demanded. The Contents were sixty-two; the Not Contents forty-seven. It was immediately proposed and carried, without a division, that the Prince and Princess of Orange should be declared King and Queen of England.

Nottingham then moved that the wording of the oaths of allegiance and supremacy should be altered in such a way that they might be conscientiously taken by persons who, like himself, disapproved of what the Convention had done, and yet fully purposed to be loyal and dutiful subjects of the new sovereigns. To his proposition no objection was made. Indeed there can be little doubt that there was an understanding on this subject between the Whig leaders and those Tory Lords whose votes had turned the scale on the last division. The new oaths were sent down to the Commons, together with the resolution that the Prince and Princess should be declared King and Queen.

It was now known to whom the crown would be given. On what conditions it should be given, still remained to be decided. The Commons had appointed a committee to consider what steps it might be advisable to take, in order to secure law and liberty against the aggressions of future sovereigns, and the committee had made a report. This report recommended, first, that those great principles of the constitution which had been violated by the dethroned King should be solemnly asserted, and, secondly, that many new laws should be enacted, for the purpose of curbing the prerogative and purifying the administration of justice. Most of the suggestions of the committee were excellent; but it was utterly impossible that the Houses could, in a month, or even in a year, deal properly with matters so numerous, so various, and so important. It was proposed, among other things, that the militia should be remodelled, that the power which the sovereign possessed or proroguing and dissolving Parliaments should be restricted; that the duration of Parliaments should be limited; that the royal pardon should not longer be pleadable to a parliamentary impeachment; that toleration should be granted to Protestant Dissenters; that the crime of high treason should be conducted in a manner more favourable to innocence; that the Judges should hold their places for life; that the mode of appointing Sheriffs should be altered; that juries should be nominated in such a way as might exclude partiality and corruption; that the practice of filing criminal informations in the King's

Bench should be abolished; that the Court of Chancery should be reformed; that the fees of public functionaries should be regulated; and that the law of Quo Warranto should be amended. It was evident that cautious and deliberate legislation on these subjects must be the work of more than one laborious session; and it was equally evident that hasty and crude legislation on subjects so grave could not but produce new grievances, worse than those which it might remove. If the committee meant to give a list of the reforms which ought to be accomplished before the throne was filled, the list was absurdly long. If, on the other hand, the committee meant to give a list of all the reforms that the legislature would do well to make in proper season, the list was strangely imperfect. Indeed, as soon as the report had been read, member after member rose to suggest some additions. It was moved and carried that the selling of offices should be prohibited, that the Habeas Corpus Act should be made more efficient, and that the law of Mandamus should be revised. One gentleman fell on the chimneymen, another on the excisemen; and the House resolved that the malpractice of both chimneymen and excisemen should be restrained. It is a most remarkable circumstance that, while the whole political, military, judicial, and fiscal system of the kingdom was thus passed in review, not a single representative of the people proposed the repeal of the statue which subjected the press to a censorship. It was not yet understood, even by the most enlightened men, that the liberty of discussion is the chief safeguard of all other liberties.

The House was greatly perplexed. Some orators vehemently said that too much time had already been lost, and that the government ought to be settled without they delay of a day

Society was unquiet: trade was languishing: the English colony in Ireland was in imminent danger of perishing: a foreign war was impending: the exiled King might, in a few weeks, be at Dublin with a French army, and from Dublin he might soon cross to Chester. Was it not insanity, at such a crisis, to leave the throne unfilled, and, while the very existence of Parliaments was in jeopardy, to waste time in debating whether Parliaments should be prorogued by the sovereign or by themselves? On the other side it was asked whether the Convention could think that it had fulfilled its mission by merely pulling down one prince and putting up another. Surely now or never was the time to secure public liberty by such fences as might effectually prevent the encroachments of prerogative. There was doubtless great weight in what was urged on both sides. The able chiefs of the Whig party, among whom Somers was fast rising to ascendancy, proposed a middle course. The House had, they said, two objects in view, which ought to be kept distinct. One object was to secure the old polity of the realm against illegal attacks: the other was to improve that polity by legal reforms. The former object might be attained by solemnly putting on record, in the resolution which called the new sovereigns to the throne, the claim of the English nation to its ancient franchises, so that the King might hold his crown, and the people their privileges, by one and the same title deed. The latter object would require a whole volume of elaborate statutes. The former object might be attained in a day: the latter, scarcely in five years. As to the former object, all parties were agreed: as to the latter, there were innumerable varieties of opinion. No member of either House would hesitate for a moment to vote that the King could not levy taxes without the consent of Parliament; but it would be hardly possible to frame any new law of procedure in cases of high treason which would not give rise to long debate, and be condemned by some persons as unjust to the prisoner, and by others as unjust to the crown. The business of an extraordinary convention of the Estates of the Realm was not to do the ordinary work of Parliaments, to regulate the fees of masters in Chancery, and to provide against the exactions of gaugers, but to put right the great machine of government. When this had been done, it would be time to inquire what improvement our institutions needed: nor would anything be risked by delay; for no sovereign who reigned merely by the choice of the nation, could long refuse his assent to any improvement which the nation, speaking through its representatives, demanded.

On these grounds the Commons wisely determined to postpone all reforms till the ancient constitution of the kingdom should have been restored in all its parts, and forthwith to fill the throne without imposing on William and Mary any other obligation than that of governing according to the existing laws of England. In order that the questions which had been in dispute between the Stuarts and the nation might never again be stirred, it was determined that the instrument by which the Prince and Princess of Orange were called to the throne, and by which the order of succession was settled, should set forth, in the most distinct and solemn manner, the fundamental principles of the constitution. This instrument, known by the name of the Declaration of Right, was prepared by a committee, of which Somers was chairman. The fact that the lowborn young barrister was appointed to so honourable and important a post in a Parliament filled with able and experienced men, only ten days after he had spoken in the House for the first time, sufficiently proves the superiority of his abilities. In a few hours the Declaration was framed and approved by the Commons. The Lords assented to it with some amendments of no great importance.

The Declaration began by recapitulating the crimes and errors which had made a revolution necessary. James had invaded the province of the legislature; had treated modest petitioning as a crime; had oppressed the Church by means of an illegal tribunal; had, without the consent of Parliament, levied taxes and maintained a standing army in time of peace; had violated the freedom of election, and perverted the course of justice. Proceedings which could lawfully be questioned only in Parliament had been made the subjects of prosecution in the King's Bench. Partial and corrupt juries had been returned: excessive bail had been required from prisoners: excessive fines had been imposed: barbarous and unusual punishments had been inflicted: the estates of accused persons had been granted away before conviction. He, by whose authority these things had been done, had abdicated the government. The Prince of Orange, whom God had made the glorious instrument of delivering the nation from superstition and tyranny, had invited the Estates of the Realm to meet and to take counsel together for the securing of religion, of law, and of freedom. The Lords and Commons, having deliberated, had resolved that they would first, after the example of their ancestors, assert the ancient rights and liberties of England. Therefore it was declared that the dispensing power, as lately assumed and exercised, had no legal existence; that, without grant of Parliament, no money could be exacted by the sovereign from the subject; that, without consent of Parliament, no standing army could be kept up in time of peace. The right of subjects to petition, the right of electors to choose representatives freely, the right of the legislature to freedom of debate, the right of the nation to a pure and merciful administration of justice according to the spirit of our mild laws, were solemnly affirmed. All these things the Convention claimed, as the undoubted inheritance of Englishmen. Having thus vindicated the principles of the constitution, the Lords and Commons, in the entire confidence that the deliverer would hold sacred the laws and liberties which he had saved, resolved that William and Mary, Prince and Princess of Orange, should be declared King and Queen of England for their joint and separate lives, and that, during their joint lives, the administration of the government should be in the Prince alone. After them the crown was settled on the posterity of Mary, then on Anne and her posterity, and then on the posterity of William.

By this time the wind had ceased to blow from the west. The ship in which the Princess of Orange had embarked lay off Margate on the eleventh of February, and, on the following morning, anchored at Greenwich. She was received with many signs of joy and affection: but her demeanour shocked the Tories, and was not thought faultless even by the Whigs. A young woman, placed, by a destiny as mournful and awful as that which brooded over the fabled houses on Labdacus and Pelops, in such a situation that she could not without violating her duty to her God, her husband, and her country, refuse to take her seat on the throne from which her father had just been hurled, should have been sad, or at least serious. Mary was not merely in high, but in extravagant, spirits. She entered Whitehall, it was asserted, with a girlish delight at being mistress of so fine a house, ran about the rooms, peeped into the closets, and examined the quilt of the state bed, without seeming to remember by whom those magnificent apartments had last been occupied. Burnet, who had, till then, thought her an angel in human form, could not, on this occasion, refrain from blaming her. He was the more astonished because, when he took leave of her at the Hague, she had, though fully convinced that she was in the path of duty, been deeply dejected. To him, as to her spiritual guide, she afterwards explained her conduct. William had written to inform her that some of those who had tried to separate her interest from his still continued their machinations: they gave it out that she thought herself wronged: and, if she wore a gloomy countenance, the report would be confirmed. He therefore entreated her to make her first appearance with an air of cheerfulness. Her heart, she said, was far indeed from cheerful; but she had done her best; and, as she was afraid of not sustaining well a part which was uncongenial to her feelings, she had overacted it. Her deportment was the subject of much spiteful prose and verse: it lowered her in the opinion of some whose esteem she valued: nor did the world know, till she was beyond the reach of praise and censure, that the conduct which had brought on her the reproach of levity and insensibility was really a signal instance of that perfect disinterestedness and selfdevotion of which man seems to be incapable, but which is sometimes found in women.

On the morning of Wednesday, the thirteenth of February, the court of Whitehall and all the neighbouring streets were filled with gazers. The magnificent Banqueting House, the masterpiece of Inigo, embellished by masterpieces of Rubens had been prepared for a great ceremony. The walls were lined by the yeomen of the guard. Near the northern door, on the right hand, a large number of Peers had assembled. On the left were the Commons with their Speaker, attended by the mace. The southern door opened: and the Prince and Princess of Orange, side by side, entered, and took their place under the canopy of state.

Both Houses approached bowing low. William and Mary advanced a few steps. Halifax on the right, and Powle on the left, stood forth; and Halifax spoke. The Convention, he said, had agreed to a resolution which he prayed Their Highnesses to hear. They signified their assent; and the clerk of the House of Lords read, in a loud voice, the Declaration of Right. When he had concluded, Halifax, in the name of all the Estates of the Realm, requested the Prince and Princess to accept the crown.

William, in his own name and in that of his wife, answered that the crown was, in their estimation, the more valuable because it was presented to them as a token of the confidence of the nation. "We thankfully accept," he said, "what you have offered us." Then, for himself, he assured them that the laws of England, which he had once already vindicated, should be the rules of his conduct, that it should be his study to promote the welfare of the kingdom, and that, as to the means of doing so, he should constantly recur to the advice of the Houses, and should be disposed to trust their judgement rather than his own. These words were received with a shout of joy which was heard in the streets below, and was instantly answered by huzzas from many thousands of voices. The Lords and Commons then reverently retired from the Banqueting House and went in procession to the great gate of Whitehall, where the heralds and pursuivants were waiting in their gorgeous tabards.

All the space as far as Charing Cross was one sea of heads. The kettle drums struck up: the trumpets pealed; and Garter King at Arms, in a loud voice, proclaimed the Prince and Princess of Orange King and Queen of England, charged all Englishmen to bear, from that moment, true allegiance to the new sovereigns, and besought God, who had already wrought to signal a deliverance for our Church and nation, to bless William and Mary with a long and happy reign.

Thus was consummated the English Revolution. When we compare it with those revolutions which have, during the last sixty years, overthrown so many ancient governments, we cannot but be struck by its peculiar character. Why that character was so peculiar is sufficiently obvious, and yet seems not to have always been understood either by eulogists or by censors.

The Continental revolutions of the eighteenth and nineteenth centuries took place in countries where all traces of the limited monarchy of the middle ages had long been effaced. The right of the prince to make laws and to levy money had, during many generations, been undisputed. His throne was guarded by a great regular army. His administration could not, without extreme peril, be blamed even in the mildest terms. His subjects held their personal liberty by no other tenure than his pleasure. Not a single institution was left which had, within the memory of the oldest man, afforded efficient protection to the subject against the utmost excess of tyranny. Those great councils which had once curbed the regal power had sunk into oblivion. Their composition and their privileges were known only to antiquaries. We cannot wonder, therefore, that, when those who had been thus ruled succeeded in wresting supreme power from a government which they had long in secret hated, they should have been impatient to demolish and unable to construct, that they should have been fascinated by every specious novelty, that they should have been proscribed every title, ceremony, and phrase associated with their old system, and that, turning away with disgust from their own national precedents and traditions, they should have sought for principles of government in the writings of theorists, or aped, with ignorant and ungraceful affectation, the patriots of Athens and Rome. As little can we wonder that the violent action of the revolutionary spirit should have been followed by reaction equally violent, and that confusion should speedily have engendered despotism sterner than that from which it had sprung.

Had we been in the same situation; had Strafford succeeded in his favourite scheme of Thorough; had he formed an army as numerous and as well disciplined as that which, a few years later, was formed by Cromwell; had a series of judicial decisions, similar to that which was pronounced by the Exchequer Chamber in the case of shipmoney, transferred to the crown the right of taxing the people; had the Star Chamber and the High Commission continued to fine mutilate, and imprison every man who dared to raise his voice against the government, had the press been as completely enslaved here as at Vienna or at Naples; had our Kings gradually drawn to themselves the whole legislative power; had six generations of Englishmen passed away without a single session of Parliament; and had we then at length risen up in some moment of wild excitement against our masters, what an outbreak would that have been! With what a crash, heard and felt to the farthest ends of the world, would the whole vast fabric of society have fallen! How many thousands of exiles, once the most prosperous and the most refined members of this great community, would have begged their bread in Continental cities, or have sheltered their heads under huts of bark in the uncleared forests of America! How often should we have seen the pavement of London piled up in barricades, the houses dinted with bullets, the gutters foaming with blood! How many times should we have rushed wildly from extreme to extreme, sought refuge from anarchy in despotism, and been again driven by despotism into anarchy! How many years of blood and confusion would it have cost us to learn the very rudiments of political science! How many childish theories would have duped us! How many rude and ill poised constitutions should we have set up, only to see them tumble down! Happy would it have been for us if a sharp discipline of half a century had sufficed to educate us into a capacity of enjoying true freedom.

These calamities our Revolution averted. It was a revolution strictly defensive, and had prescription and legitimacy on its side. Here, and here only, a limited monarchy of the thirteenth century had come down unimpaired to the seventeenth century. Our parliamentary institutions were in full vigour. The main principles of our government were excellent. They were not, indeed, formally and exactly set forth in a single written instrument; but they were to be found scattered over our ancient and noble statutes; and, what was of far greater moment, they had been engraven on the hearts of Englishmen during four hundred years. that, without the consent of the representatives of the nation, no legislative act could be passed, no tax imposed, no regular soldiery kept up, that no man could be imprisoned, even for a day, by the arbitrary will of the sovereign, that no tool of power could plead the royal command as a justification for violating any right of the humblest subject, were held, both by Whigs and Tories, to be fundamental laws of the realm. A realm of which these were the fundamental laws stood in no need of a new constitution.

But, though a new constitution was not needed, it was plain that changes were required. The misgovernment of the Stuarts, and the troubles which that misgovernment had produced, sufficiently proved that there was somewhere a defect in our polity; and that defect it was the duty of the Convention to discover and to supply.

Some questions of great moment were still open to dispute. Our constitution had begun to exist in times when statesmen were not much accustomed to frame exact definitions. Anomalies, therefore, inconsistent with its principles and dangerous to its very existence, had sprung up almost imperceptibly, and, not having, during many years, caused any serious inconvenience, had gradually acquired the force of prescription. The remedy for these evils was to assert the rights of the people in such language as should terminate all controversy, and to declare that no precedent could justify any violation of those rights.

When this had been done it would be impossible for our rulers to misunderstand the law: but, unless something more were done, it was by no means improbable that they might violate it. Unhappily the Church had long taught the nation that hereditary monarchy, alone among our institutions, was divine and inviolable; that the right of the House of Commons to a share in the legislative power was a right merely human, but that the right of the King to the obedience of his people was from above; that the Great Charter was a statute which might be repealed by those who had made it, but that the rule which called the princes of the blood royal to the throne in order of succession was of celestial origin, and that any Act of Parliament, inconsistent with that rule was a nullity. It is evident that, in a society in which such superstitions prevail, constitutional freedom must ever be insecure. A power which is regarded merely as the ordinance of man cannot be an efficient check on a power which is regarded as the ordinance of God. It is vain to hope that laws, however excellent, will permanently restrain a king who, in his own opinion, and in the opinion of a great part of his people, has an authority infinitely higher in kind than the authority which belongs to those laws. To deprive royalty of these mysterious attributes, and to establish the principle that Kings reigned by a right in no respect differing from the right by which freeholders chose knights of the shire, or from the right by which Judges granted writs of Habeas Corpus, was absolutely necessary to the security of our liberties.

Thus the Convention had two great duties to perform. The first was to clear the fundamental laws of the realm from ambiguity. The second was to eradicate from the minds, both of the governors and of the governed, the false and pernicious notion that the royal prerogative was something more sublime and holy than those fundamental laws. The former object was attained by the solemn recital and claim with which the Declaration of Right commences; the latter by the resolution which pronounced the throne vacant, and invited William and Mary to fill it.

The change seems small. Not a single flower of the crown

was touched. Not a single new right was given to the people. The whole English law, substantive and adjective, was, in the judgement of all the greatest lawyers, of Holt and Treby, of Maynard and Somers, almost exactly the same after the Revolution as before it. Some controverted points had been decided according to the sense of the best jurists; and there had been a slight deviation from the ordinary course of succession. This was all; and this was enough.

As our Revolution was a vindication of ancient rights, so it was conducted with strict attention to ancient formalities. In almost every word and act may be discerned a profound reverence for the past. The Estates of the Realm deliberated in the old halls and according to the old rules. Powle was conducted to his chair between his mover and his seconder with the accustomed forms. The Serjeant with his mace brought up the messengers of the Lords to the table of the Commons; and the three obeisances were duly made. The conference was held with all the antique ceremonial. On one side of the table, in the Painted Chamber, the managers for the Lords sate covered and robed in ermine and gold. The managers for the Commons stood bareheaded on the other side. The speeches present an almost ludicrous contrast to the revolutionary oratory of every other country. Both the English parties agreed in treating with solemn respect the ancient constitutional traditions of the state. The only question was, in what sense those traditions were to be understood. The assertors of liberty said not a word about the natural equality of men and the inalienable sovereignty of the people, about Harmodius or Timoleon, Brutus the elder or Brutus the younger. When they were told that, by the English law, the crown, at the moment of a demise, must descend to the next heir, they answered that, by the English law, a living man could have no heir. When they were told that there was no precedent for declaring the throne vacant, they produced from among the records in the Tower a roll of parchment, near three hundred years old, on which, in quaint characters and barbarous Latin, it was recorded that the Estates of the Realm had declared vacant the throne of a perfidious and tyrannical Plantagenet. When at length the dispute had been accommodated, the new sovereigns were proclaimed with the old pageantry. All the fantastic pomp of heraldry was there, Clarencieux and Norroy, Portcullis and Rouge Dragon, the trumpets, the banners, the grotesque coats embroidered with lions and lilies. The title of King of France, assumed by the conqueror of Cressy, was not omitted in the royal style. To us, who have lived in the year 1848, it may seem almost an abuse of terms to call a proceeding, conducted with so much deliberation, with so much sobriety, and with such minute attention to prescriptive etiquette, by the terrible name of Revolution.

And yet this revolution, of all revolutions the least violent, has been of all revolutions the most beneficent. It finally decided the great question whether the popular element which had, ever since the age of Fitzwalter and De Montfort, been found in the English polity, should be destroyed by the monarchical element, or should be suffered to develope itself freely, and to become dominant. The strife between the two principles has been long, fierce and doubtful. It had lasted through four reigns. It had produced seditions, impeachments, rebellions, battles, sieges, proscriptions, judicial massacres. Sometimes liberty, sometimes royalty, had seemed to be on the point of perishing. During many years one half of the energy of England had been employed in counteracting the other half. The executive power and the legislative power had so effectually impeded each other that the state had been of no account in Europe. The King at Arms, who proclaimed William and Mary before Whitehall Gate, did in truth announce that this great struggle was over; that there was entire union between the throne and Parliament; that England, long dependent and degraded, was again a power of the first rank; that the ancient laws by which the prerogative was bounded would thenceforth be held as sacred as the prerogative itself, and would be followed out to all their consequences; that the executive administration would be conducted in conformity with the sense of the representatives of the nation; and that no reform, which the two Houses should, after mature deliberation, propose, would be obstinately withstood by the sovereign. The Declaration of Right, though it made nothing law which had not been law before, contained the germ of the law which gave religious freedom to the Dissenter, of the law which secured the independence of the judges, of the law which limited the duration of Parliaments, of the law which placed the liberty of the press under the projection of juries, of the law which prohibited the slave trade, of the law which abolished the sacramental test, of the law which relieved the Roman Catholics from civil disabilities, of the law which reformed the representative system, of every good law which has been passed during more than a century and a half, of every good law which may hereafter, in the course of ages, be found necessary to promote the public weal, and to satisfy the demands of public opinion.

The highest eulogy which can be pronounced on the

revolution of 1688 is this, that it was our last revolution. Several generations have now passed away since any wise and patriotic Englishman has meditated resistance to the established government. In all honest and reflecting minds there is a conviction, daily strengthened by experience, that the means of effecting every improvement which the constitution requires may be found within the constitution itself.

Now, if ever, we ought to be able to appreciate the whole importance of the stand which was made by our forefathers against the House of Stuart. All around us the world is convulsed by the agonies of great nations. Governments which lately seemed likely to stand during ages have been on a sudden shaken and overthrown. The proudest capitals of Western Europe have streamed with civil blood. All evil passions, the thirst of gain, and the thirst of vengeance, the antipathy of class to class, the antipathy of race to race, have broken loose from the control of divine and human laws. Fear and anxiety have clouded the faces and depressed the hearts of millions. Trade has been suspended, and industry paralysed. The rich have become poor; and the poor have become poorer. Doctrines hostile to all sciences, to all arts, to all industry, to all domestic charities, doctrines which, if carried into effect, would, in thirty years, undo all that thirty centuries have done for mankind, and would make the fairest provinces of France and Germany as savage as Congo or Patagonia, have been avowed from the tribune and defended by the sword. Europe has been threatened with subjugation by barbarians, compared with whom the barbarians who marched under Attila and Alboin were enlightened and humane. The truest friends of the people have with deep sorrow owned that interests more precious than any political privileges were in jeopardy, and that it might be necessary to sacrifice even liberty in order to save civilisation. Meanwhile in our island the regular course of government has never been for a day interrupted. The few bad men who longed for license and plunder have not had the courage to confront for one moment the strength of a loyal nation, rallied in firm array round a parental throne. And, if it be asked what has made us to differ from others, the answer is that we never lost what others are wildly and blindly seeking to regain. It is because we had a preserving revolution in the seventeenth century that we have not had a destroying revolution in the nineteenth. It is because we had freedom in the midst of servitude that we have order in the midst of anarchy. For the authority of law, for the security of property, for the peace of our streets, for the happiness of our homes, our gratitude is due, under Him who raises and pulls down nations at his pleasure, to the Long Parliament, to the Convention, and to William of Orange.

NOTES

1. Barillon, the French Ambassador.

2. The King's Jesuit confessor.

3. Earl of Sunderland, James' closest advisor and minister.

4. James' first marriage was to Anne Hyde, who bore him the Princess Mary, married to William of Orange, and Anne. The current head of the Hyde family, the Earl of Clarendon, was a minister and a Privy Councillor who often appears in Macaulay's pages.

5. Thomas Sprat, Dean of Westminster and Bishop of Rochester.

6. 'thirtieth of January', 'twenty-ninth of May' were respectively the dates of Charles I's execution, and the return of Charles II to London from exile in 1660.

7. A Puritan agitator for whom Macaulay had a particular aversion. He took a leading part in the Monmouth Rebellion.

8. Burnet was a Whig clergyman who favoured toleration. He resided in the Hague and joined William's invasion. Macaulay uses him as a source.

9. The regiment of Colonel Kirke had distinguished itself by atrocities in the suppression of Monmouth's Rebellion. The regimental badge was a paschal lamb.

10. The royal commander in chief.

11. Earl of Melfort, James' minister in Scotland. He converted to Catholicism and shared the King's exile.